IP for EVERYONE

IN TIME

(THE TIMELINES)

From An Indian Perspective

Part -II

IP for EVERYONE

IN TIME

(THE TIMELINES)

From An Indian Perspective

Part -II

By

Pranav Chaturvedi

Vij Books

New Delhi (India)

Published by

Vij Books
(Publishers, Distributors & Importers)
4836/24, Ansari Road
Delhi – 110 002
Phone: 91-11-43596460
Mobile: 98110 94883
e-mail: contact@vijpublishing.com
www.vijbooks.in

ISBN: 978-81-19438-39-6 (Paperback)

Dedicated to My Parents

Late Dr. Rabindra Nath Chaturvedi
&
Late Mrs. Shashi Chaturvedi

Contents

The Timelines

The Author's earlier book, *IP For EVERYONE: Ethics, Filing, Reflections, From An Indian Perspective,* discussed core concepts of the Intellectual Property Rights (Patents, Trademarks, Copyrights, Designs, G.I., Domain Name Disputes) and also covered its ethical dilemmas & reflections, in the language as condensed as possible, covering all the important aspects of IPR from an Indian perspective, that can be read and used by everyone. It neither covered nor included many case precedence for the reason because the conclusions made by different courts and registries are complex to understand. What was covered in the book was a highly condensed form with respect to preliminary and the intermediate stages of filing at different offices.

Whereas, the present book, *IP For Everyone, IN TIME, The TIMELINES, From An Indian Perspective - Part -II*, is restricted to the *Timelines* that discusses the timelines in IPR from the lens of the Applicant, Opponent, Person Aggrieved, Complainant, and Respondent. With the help of these timelines, one can understand the statutory period to initiate an action or a response with regards to IPR in India as well as at WIPO.

The timelines are subject to change, however, at the time this book is being written, the author has tried to include the updated information about the timelines to the best of his knowledge and belief.

The author has tried to summarize the illustrious timelines and time schedule in a simple format; alike the previous book that discusses the ethics, filing procedures and dilemmas in IPR, for everyone.

Patent Timelines

Filing of the Patent Application

Any time as soon as the invention is either fully developed, or partially equipped with, then:

> ➢ File Complete Specification directly, if wholly conceptualized/ materialized.

> ➢ If not, file Provisional Specification (application), and then within **12 Months,** file Complete Specification. If within **12 Months** from the date of filing of the provisional specification, the complete specification is not filed, then the application would be treated as **abandoned**.

> ➢ The Forms included would be FORM 1 (Form of Application For The Grant Of Patent), FORM 2 (Provisional / Complete Specification), FORM 3 (Information & Undertaking Regarding Foreign Application u/s 8), FORM 5 (Declaration as to Inventorship), FORM 9 (Optional for Early Publication), FORM 18/18A (Request for Examination / Expedited Examination), FORM 26 (General Power of Attorney For The Agent On Record), FORM 30 (If No Other FORM Is Available).

> ➢ If FORM 5 (Declaration as to Inventorship) is not filed with Complete Specification & the Form of Application for The Grant of Patent, then within **1 Month** from the date of filing of the Complete Specification, it may be filed, if an application is made in FORM 4 seeking extension, and if the controller deems fit.

> ➢ In any case, once the application for the patent is filed, then it would be published within **18 Months** from the date of filing or priority, whichever is earlier. Yet, if the applicant seeks early publication, then it can file FORM 9 as Request for Publication, then the application will be published within **1 Month** from the date of request under Rule 24-A of the Patent Rules. One thing

to be noted is that under rule 55 (1-A), no patent shall be granted before **6 Months** from the date of publication u/s (under section) 11-A, as mentioned above.

➢ FORM 18 (Request for the Examination) can be filed within **31 Months** (earlier it was **48 Months**) from the date of priority or date of filing whichever is earlier / or within **6 Months** from the date of revocation of the secrecy direction / within **6 Months** from the date of filing of the further application, whichever is later.

➢ Examiner shall make report u/s 12(2) within **1 Month** but not exceeding **3 Months** once reference of the application for examination has been received from the Controller. The Controller shall dispose of report by the examiner within **1 Month.**

➢ First statement of objections shall be issued by the Controller to the Applicant within **1 Month** from the date of disposal of report of examiner by the Controller.

➢ Time for putting an application for grant u/s 21 is **6 Months** which can be further extended upto **3 Months** if a request has been made by the Applicant. The process has already been discussed in the previous book whilst elaborating on how to file the Reply to FER or Written Submissions along with the cogent documents as necessary.

➢ For the *Expedited Examination*, an application can be made in FORM 18A only on the following grounds that Applicant is:

1. Startup;

2. Small Entity;

3. At least one of the Applicant is female in case of natural person(s), jointly or severely;

4. Department of government;

5. Institution wholly or substantially financed by the government;

6. Government company as defined u/s 2 (45) of companies act, 2013;

7. Has elected India as IPEA or indicated India as ISA in the International Application.

A request for expedited examination should be filed with request for publication u/r (under rule) 24A as discussed above, that is for the early publication of the application within **1 Month**. Examiner shall thus make report u/s 12(2) within **1 Month** but not exceeding **2 Months** once the reference of application for examination has been received from the controller. The time wherein the Controller shall dispose of report by the examiner, shall be **1 Month.**

First statement of objections (FER) shall be issued by the Controller to the Applicant within **15 days** from the date of disposal of report of examiner by the Controller. Time for putting the application for grant is **6 Months** which can be further extended upto **3 Months** if a request on FORM 4 has been made by the Applicant. The Controller shall dispose of the application within a period of **3 Months** from the date of Reply received from the Applicant, or, within a period of **3 Months** from the last date to put application in order for grant.

There're certain guidelines that needs to be addressed while filing the document and copies etc. at the patent office which should be typewritten either in Hindi or English along with legible characters, on a durable white A4 paper, wherein on right half of left margin, it should contain *numbers* at every **5**[th] consecutive lines, i.e., in multiples of 5, 10, 15, 20......, along with the applicant's / agent's signatures at the appropriate places. The names, addresses, nationalities of the applicants', along with that of the inventors shall be filed in the appropriate offices at the time of filing of the patent application in all the Forms. Furthermore, wherein a patent agent files a patent application, then he/she shall file all the documents, as already discussed in the previous section, after creating an account on the IP portal; and if in case any original document is asked to be submitted, then one has to file that document within a specified period from the date of such instructions or communications; else it would be assumed that those documents be deemed *not* to have been filed.

Patent of Addition, means, an application of improvements made in the invention (i.e. in the complete specification already filed). But shouldn't be filed **Before** filing of the main invention i.e. of the complete specification; and the date of filing of which should be either **Same or Later** of the filing date of the main invention. A Patent of Addition is **not** granted **Before** grant of Patent of the Main Invention. Its term would be the **Equal** to that of the main invention. And if the main invention has been revoked, then the court or the controller can make patent of addition independent on request of the applicant, the term of which will be the remaining term of the main invention. No renewal fees has to be paid for patent of addition.

Withdrawal of the application can be made any time **after filing of the application or before the grant of the patent**.

Anticipation i.e. the period within which the Application can be filed by the Applicant after the invention has been publicly displayed with certain limitation viz. for the purpose of industrial exhibition; or, before any learned society or published with the inventor's consent in transaction of such society; or, if the invention has been displayed or used at any exhibition without the inventor's consent; then that invention can be filed no later than **12 Months** after opening of the exhibition or publication or reading.

Statement and Undertaking regarding the foreign application u/r 12(2) & u/s 8(1)(b) shall be filed within **3 Months** from the date of the first statement of objections issued u/r 24B(3) / 24C(8); and in case of the Controller's instructions u/s 8(2), then within **2 Months** for furnishing a fresh statement and undertaking.

Whereas, the applicant has to file the statement and undertaking regarding foreign applications u/s 8(1) within **6 Months** from the filing of the application. Thus, there're multiple scenarios about the statement and undertaking wherein the timelines are being mentioned above.

As the term of the patent is **20 Years**, thus, if in case the patent has been granted, then the applicant has to renew the patent from **3rd Year** onwards from the date of filing of the patent upto the life cycle of the patent, every year. And if in case the principal patent is granted **more than 2 Years** from the date of filing of the patent, then, whatever the fees is pending, can be made, within a period of **3 Months** from the date when which the grant of patent has been recorded in the register. This **3 Months** period can be extended upto **6 Months** but that should not be later than **9 Months in total** from the date of recording of the patent grant.

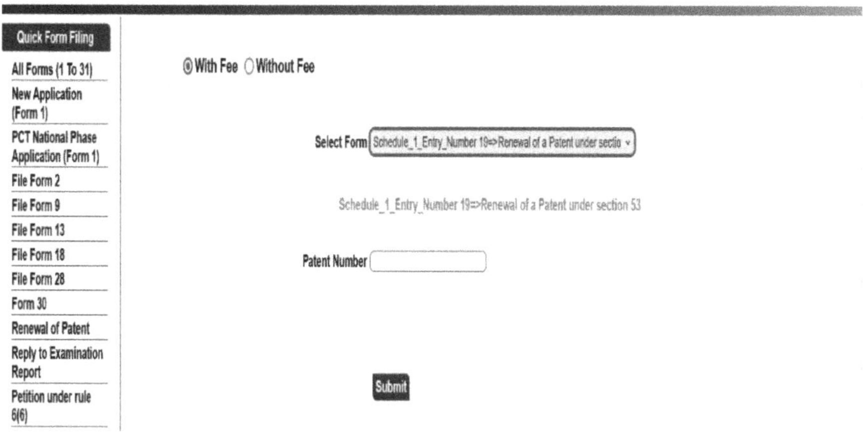

https://ipronline.ipindia.gov.in/epatentfiling/FORM30/frmFORM30MENU.aspx

If in case the patent has been granted, then the certificate of the patent shall be issued within **7 Days** u/r 74(2) from the date of grant of the patent.

Restoration

Let's say the renewal fees hasn't been paid by the patentee and the patent granted has been ceased, then, an application to restore the patent can be filed within **18 Months** from the date when the patent granted ceased or lapsed. Such an application shall mention the genuine and valid reasons as why the patent lapsed shall be restored further giving such evidence via cogent exhibits, as may be necessary, as what led to the failure to pay the prescribed fee in time.

As stated under Section 39, a permission to make the patent outside India shall be made in FORM 25 and an application has been made within India, and not less than within the period of **6 Weeks** before an application has been made outside India; and the controller has to dispose of that application within a period of **21 Days** from the date of filing of such application.

When the secrecy directions are being imposed on any of the patent application, then such directions have been reviewed periodically and these are being reconsidered every **6 Months** by the central government or on the request made by the applicant u/s 36(1). And when such reconsideration application has been filed by the applicant u/s 36(2), then u/r 72, the result of the decision of the controller shall be communicated to the applicant within a period of **15 Days**.

At times, the proof of right is accompanied by the patent application, i.e., when the Patent has been acquired via assignment & an application for the patent has been made under that right, then such proof of right needs to be submitted either with the application or within **6 Months** from the date of filing of the application.

In case there's a situation of anticipation by prior claiming, and that objection is still withstanding, then the controller can postpone the grant of the patent and give **2 Months** of time for removing such objections, and once the objections are being removed, then the patent can follow for further proceedings. And if the objections have not been removed, then the controller can appoint a hearing, either when the applicant requests for it, or by the controller itself, and after the hearing, then instruct the applicant to remove the objections. For the hearing, the controller would give at least **10 Days** of notice to the applicant of the hearing date so fixed. And the applicant needs to notify the Controller as soon as possible but not later than **3 Days** from the date of hearing.

Surrender of Patents

Let's say, the patentee wants or offers to surrender the patent at any time, then the controller would publish such an offer and would notify every other person whose names appear other than the name of the patentee, wherein such person can file notice of opposition to such offer of surrendering within **3 Months** from the date of publication of such notice. After hearing both the sides, if any, the controller may revoke the patent. Herein also, the provision of rules 57 to 63 as discussed would be applicable.

Information Regarding Working of Patent

The controller has the power to call for information from the patentees/ licensees when the patent is effective and within **2 Months** from the date of such notice, the patentee or the licensee has to submit in detail such information or such periodical statements w.r.t. how and where the *patented invention has been worked*. Remember, a patented invention needs to be worked in India, or else as discussed herein below or in the earlier book, a compulsory license can be issued, or, the patented invention can even be revoked. Further, patentee and licensee have to furnish in 6 Months (extended by upto 3 Months) w.r.t. every 3 Financial Years from date of grant. (S. 146 & R. 131).

Authorization of Agent

When a patent agent is hired, then within the period of **3 Months** from the date of filing of the application or document; the authorization of the agent shall be submitted, in the form of power of attorney/GPA.

Hearing

If the written submissions made in the Reply to the FER has been accepted, then Patent grant order would be issued.

*|If not, a chance of hearing would be provided to the Applicant, of which the Applicant has to notify to the controller at least **usually 3 Days** prior to the hearing date u/r 28(4) whether he/she would or wouldn't attend the hearing.*

*A written submission can be filed within **15 Days** from the **date of first hearing**. If even after the hearing, the order of the controller isn't acceptable to the Applicant, then the Applicant can file a Review petition within **1 Month** from the date of communication of the decision, that can be extended upto not more than **1 more Month** if request made on FORM 4 for extension. (Rule 130/ u/s 77(1)(f) and (g)).*

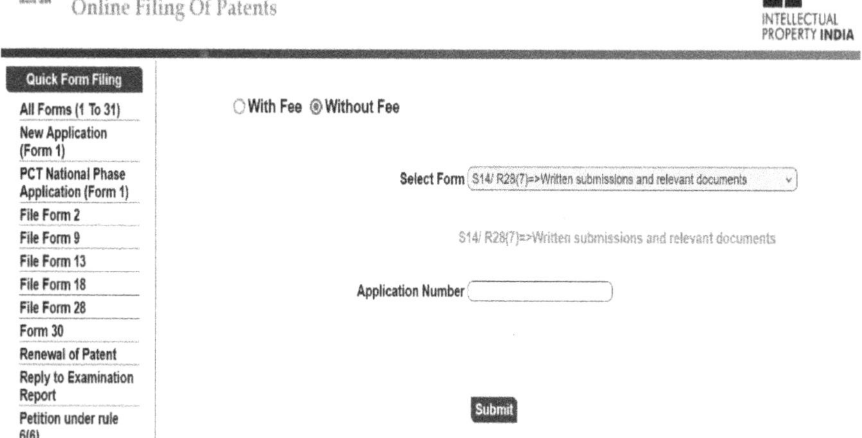

https://ipronline.ipindia.gov.in/epatentfiling/FORM30/frmFORM30MENU.aspx|

*If the controller pass an ex-parte order, on the occasions when, let's say, Applicant didn't appear for the hearing nor submitted the Written Submission with **15 Days** from the date of hearing; then to set-aside such orders, a review petition can be filed, within **1 Month** from the date of such order, and that time period can be extended by **1 Month** if an application has been made for extension on **FORM 4.***

*If the Applicant seeks adjournment of the hearing, then the applicant may make a request for adjournment at least **3 Days** before the date of hearing to the controller. A reasonable cause needs to be written in the adjournment application. No more than **2 Adjournments** shall be given by the controller to the applicant. Each adjournment shall not be more than of **30 Days**.*

One thing to be noted is that if a request of extension for time to file review petition has been filed as stated above, it should be accompanied by Statements setting forth the grounds on which the application is based.

Patent Agents

Regarding Patent Agents who are authorized to file & attend any proceedings in front of the patents & designs offices and via whom, usually if taken professional help, any patent application or opposition or other proceedings has been filed, such patent agents need to file Renewal Fee **Every Year** for the continuance of his/her name in the register.

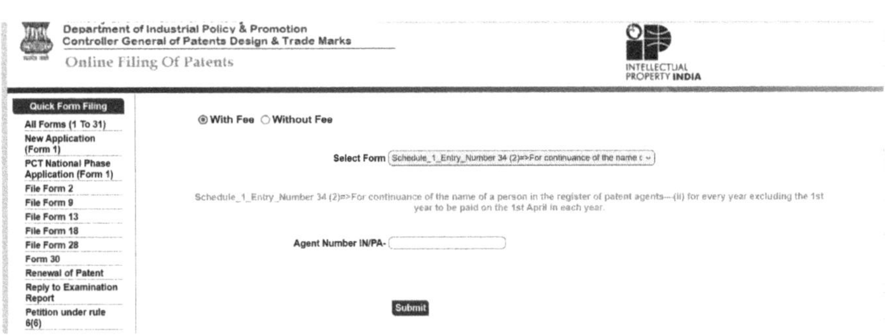

Department of Industrial Policy & Promotion
Controller General of Patents Design & Trade Marks
Online Filing Of Patents

INTELLECTUAL PROPERTY INDIA

Quick Form Filing
All Forms (1 To 31)
New Application (Form 1)
PCT National Phase Application (Form 1)
File Form 2
File Form 9
File Form 13
File Form 18
File Form 28
Form 30
Renewal of Patent
Reply to Examination Report
Petition under rule 6(6)

With Fee   Without Fee

Select Form   Schedule_1_Entry_Number 34 (2)=>For continuance of the name c

Schedule_1_Entry_Number 34 (2)=>For continuance of the name of a person in the register of patent agents—(ii) for every year excluding the 1st year to be paid on the 1st April in each year.

Agent Number IN/PA-

Submit

https://ipronline.ipindia.gov.in/epatentfiling/FORM30/frmFORM30MENU.aspx

The name of the patent agent can be restored in the register within **2 Months** from the date of such removal. If the name is restored, then it would be communicated to the patent agent and also would be published on the official website. One can check online the list of all patent agents on the Indian IP Portal, who're valid and subsisting, their official addresses and contact emails. The renewal shall be for a period of **1 Year** as the patent agent has to pay the annual renewal fee to remain in the register of patent agents in the IP Office.

For filing of the patent agent continuance fee or renewal of the patent or the patent application or opposition or the PCT application designated India, all these can be made on the online portal of www.ipindia.gov.in, and one can avail the facility.

Opposition

Pre-Grant Opposition

Anywhere between when the application of the patent has been published, to, before the grant of the patent, any person aggrieved or who has a locus standi can in writing file an opposition. The grounds should be restricted to but not limited to:

- ➢ *Applicant wrongfully obtained the patent from him or under whom through he claims;*

- ➢ *Invention has already been published before the priority;*

- ➢ *Invention claimed has been publicly known or used before priority;*

- ➢ *Invention is obvious & does not involve inventive steps;*

- ➢ *Invention isn't an invention within the meaning of Section 3;*

- ➢ *Information hasn't been disclosed under section 8;*

- ➢ *Convention application hasn't been made within **12 Months**;*

- ➢ *Invention wrongly discloses the origin of the biological material.*

Post-Grant Opposition

Anywhere after the grant of any patent but before expiry of a 1 Year period from the date of publication of grant in the journal, any person aggrieved or who has a locus standi can in writing file an opposition. The grounds would be same as mentioned above in the Pre-Grant section.

Once the opposition has been received, especially under the *Post-Grant*, the controller shall constitute an opposition board and they would examine the case, and eventually both sides would be given an opportunity

& accordingly, patent shall either be amended or revoked or maintain the status-quo.

The opposition shall include the statements and the evidence, in support of the application, and also a request of the hearing too, if desired.

https://ipronline.ipindia.gov.in/epatentfiling/OnlineFiling/OnlineFiling

No representation for pre-grant opposition can be considered unless the applicant has filed request for Examination in FORM 18/18A within the stipulated period of time as mentioned above.

FORM 7 as Notice of Opposition to Post-Grant, and FORM 7A for Representation of Opposition to Pre-Grant.

*If there's no prima facie case in the representation of the opposition, and unless the opponent requests to be heard on the said matter, then within **1 Month** the controller shall pass an order the grounds of refusal; or within **1 Month** from the date of hearing, pass an order of refusal or prima facie acceptance of representation of opposition.*

*And if in case there's prima facie case is made out, then within **1 Month** from the date of receiving the representation, notify the applicant.*

*The applicant in case of Representation of the Opposition can file statements & evidence in support of his application within **2 Months** from the date of such notice.*

The controller may either reject thereafter the representation, or, ask the applicant to amend the specification itself before the patent is granted, or, refuse to grant a patent on the application, within **1 Month** from the completion of the above proceedings.

The timeline for rest of the hearing would depend & will be followed according to Rule 62(2) to 62(4).

If either party wants to be heard, then they shall notify the controller in advance

The controller may refuse to hear any party who has not given a notice in advance

And if either of the party intends to rely on the hearing that hasn't been included in the submitted documents in the above proceedings, then no less than **5 Days** notice shall be given by that party to all the sides along with the details of such publication

The controller shall give the parties of the hearing no less than **10 Days** of notice for the hearing. And if say either of the party wants to rely on any publication, as mentioned above, and what wasn't been included or mentioned in the notice or statement or evidence, then in that scenario, that party needs to give notice to the other side as well as to the controller, no less than **5 Days** of the notice of its intention and the details of such publication.

In case of the Post-Grant opposition u/s 25(2) and as stated above, the opposition board is constituted, in the case if the opposition is filed within **1 Year** from the date of the grant of the patent i.e. publication of the grant of patent. The grounds on which such opposition can be filed has already been mentioned in the above section. Once the opposition board is constituted by the controller, it shall conduct the examination of the notice of opposition along with the documents submitted by the opponent and the patentee u/r 57-60, & submits its report & recommendations with reasons within **2 Months** from the date on which the documents were forwarded to them.

As stated above, u/r 57-60, the opponents need to send that written statement & evidence in support of the opposition to the patentee.

If the patentee desires to counter the opposition, it shall send the reply to the written statement along with the cogent evidence within the period of **2 Months** from the date of receipt of the copy of the written statements and evidence received from the opponent and deliver it to the opponent and to the Controller as well.

Now, if the patentee does not desire to adduce any evidence in support of its patent, then it would be considered as if the patent had already been revoked.

The opponent thereafter if in case the patentee has filed his/her evidence shall file the Reply to the statements and evidence filed by the patentee within **1 Month**, *which would be strictly restricted to the evidence and statements filed by the applicant.*

No further evidence shall be filed by either side unless taken the leave of the controller. Once this cycle of receiving the recommendation & reasons from the board & on completion of presentation of the evidences as stated earlier, the controller shall fix a date of hearing and would give no less than **10 Days** *of such hearing and may require the opposition board to be present at the time of hearing.*

The controller may pass this order on the reasonable grounds and would notify to all the parties.

If in case the patentee wants to withdraw the patent after the notice of opposition, then the controller may decide whether to award cost or not to the opponent.

Now, a request can also be made by the opponent u/s 26(1) within **3 Months** *if in case the opponent seeks that the patent should be granted in favour of the opponent from the date of the order of the controller, that should also contain the statements and facts and relief claimed.*

As we've seen above, the process of the opposition proceedings is almost same for the pre-grant opposition and for the post-grant opposition as well, which are followed under the Rules 57-62 as discussed above.

Amendments

The Amendments can be carried out in the patent application, be it in the complete specification or any other document, after the grant of patent, which would be published in the journal. And if there're any substantive changes and if any person wants to oppose such amendments, then that person can oppose within **3 Months** from the date of publication of the application with the respective amendments. In this case too, the rules from 57 to 63 would be applicable for the disposal of such opposition. (R. 81)

Compulsory License

There is another provision of compulsory license which can be granted to the party interested or one who has locus-standi, at any time after the *expiry* of **3 Years** from the date of the grant of the patent. The grounds of the compulsory license should be restricted to:

- ➢ reasonable requirement of public hasn't been met;
- ➢ at a reasonable price the patent invention is not available;
- ➢ the invention for which the patent has been granted hasn't worked in India;

A patent can also be revoked by the controller for non-working in case the compulsory license has been granted and after the expiration of **2 Years** from the date of order granting of the first compulsory license, any interested person can apply to the controller for ordering of the revocation of the patent for the reasons as stated above. Such application would be decided within the period of **1 Year** from being presented to the Controller. (S.85)

The applicant for the compulsory license must make certain efforts to obtain the license of the patent from the patentee on certain reasonable terms & conditions & the reasonable time that the applicant should try shall ordinarily not be exceeding **6 Months**, before making an application for the compulsory license.

The life-cycle of the proceeding of the compulsory license would be:

*if prima facie case is not made, the controller shall notify the applicant within **1 Month** from the date of such notification, and refuse the application for the compulsory license*

If prima-facie case is made out, then the applicant would serve the copies to the patentee

*Patentee or any other person desiring to oppose can oppose the application within a period of **2 Months** from the date of publication of the application u/s 87(1) along with the evidence*

No further statement or evidence would be allowed unless taken leave from the controller

*Hearing; and no less than **10 Days** of notice would be given to the parties concerned* *u/r 62(2)-62(5) shall be applicable for the procedure for hearing*

Wherein the terms and conditions of the license are settled by the controller, the licensee, if he/she has worked the invention on the commercial scale for a period of no less than **12 Months**, can file for a revision of the terms & conditions if it feels the original settled terms & conditions were more onerous & the licensee is going under the loss. This must be remembered that no such application for the revision of the terms & conditions would be accepted or entertained by the controller **2ⁿᵈ Time** (S.88(4)).

The compulsory license can also be terminated by the controller if in case of an application received from the patentee or any other person deriving title from the same, if in case the grounds or circumstances on which the compulsory license was granted no longer exists or unlikely to occur. In such a situation, the holder of the compulsory license shall have the right to object to such termination.

The application for the termination of the compulsory license u/s 94 can be made by the patentee or any other person deriving the title or interest of the same.

The applicant shall serve such copy to the holder of the compulsory license & inform to the controller.

*The holder of the compulsory license shall file whatsoever objections against such application and shall file a reply along with the evidence within **1 Month** from the date of receipt of the application.*

*No further evidence shall be filed unless taken leave from the controller. The controller shall fix a date of the hearing and would give no less than **10 Days** of notice for the same. Again, the procedure of the rule 62(2) to 62(5) shall be applicable, as seen in the other hearing proceedings as well.*

Condonation of Delay

The date of a notice or written communication addressed to a patentee or applicant or opponent shall be the date of the dispatch by registered post or speed post or fax or by electronic transmission duly authenticated. And in case of a delay in receipt of the document or communication sent by the patent office to the applicant or the patentee or to any other person interested or involved, then the delay in transmitting or resubmitting a document to the patent office shall be condoned by the controller, provided that a petition for the condonation of delay needs to be filed immediately after the receipt of such document providing the circumstances of the facts involved.

The controller may **condone the delay** w.r.t submitting the documents to the patent office if in case in an area where the applicant resides has been subjected to war, revolution, civil disorder, strike, natural calamity, general unavailability of the electronic communication services or other alike reason, wherein the relevant action should be taken as soon as the situation was subsided, and the period within which the relevant action was taken was not more than **1 Month** from the date when such situation ceased to exist.

Furthermore, the controller, in case of national emergency was in force, shall not exceed the period of condonation of delay for which the national emergency was in force or **6 Months** from the date of expiry of such period u/r 6(6), whichever is earlier.

Under Rule 138, the controller has powers to extend the timeline. Thence, that time limit can be extended or condoned by a period of upto **6 Months**; again, if the request of extension has been made in FORM 4.

In case of the statement & undertaking u/s 8, the controller may condone the delay for upto **3 Months** if request is made in FORM 4. (R.12(5))

The Controller may also direct the applicant to furnish the statement and undertaking regarding foreign application within the period of **2 Months** from the date of such hearing.

In the recent example of the Covid Era cum Biowarfare, the timeline to file any of the required documents or to initiate the proceedings, were being *extended* with the limitation period of almost **2 Years**; as from **15/03/2020** to **28/02/2022** were excluded from the limitation act for all the judicial and quasi-judicial proceedings and the balance period was available from the date of **01/03/2022**. And in the case wherein the limitation period would've expired between the above dates i.e. between **15/03/2020** to **28/02/2022**, then all the persons were given limitation period of **90 Days** from **01/03/2022**. And in case, the actual balance period of the limitation was more than **90 Days,** then that longer period would've applied.

5. Taking into consideration the arguments advanced by learned counsel and the impact of the surge of the virus on public health and adversities faced by litigants in the prevailing conditions, we deem it appropriate to dispose of the M.A. No. 21 of 2022 with the following directions:

    I. The order dated 23.03.2020 is restored and in continuation of the subsequent orders dated 08.03.2021, 27.04.2021 and 23.09.2021, it is directed that the period from 15.03.2020 till 28.02.2022 shall stand excluded for the purposes of limitation as may be prescribed under any general or special laws in respect of all judicial or quasi-judicial proceedings.

    II. Consequently, the balance period of limitation remaining as on 03.10.2021, if any, shall become available with effect from 01.03.2022.

    III. In cases where the limitation would have expired during the period between 15.03.2020 till 28.02.2022, notwithstanding the actual balance period of limitation remaining, all persons shall have a limitation period of 90 days from 01.03.2022. In the event the actual balance period of limitation remaining, with effect from 01.03.2022 is greater than 90 days, that longer period shall apply...."

It is accordingly notified to all the concerned stakeholders/litigants that the period of limitation shall be computed in accordance with the afore-cited order dated 10.01.2022 (enclosed) passed by the Hon'ble Supreme Court of India.

Sd/-

https://ipindia.gov.in/writereaddata/Portal/News/784_1_Public_Notice_dated_18th_January_2022_for_publication_on_website.pdf

International Applications

As discussed in the earlier book, there are two ways to file a patent application for international protection. Within **12 Months** after filing of the basic application, i.e., the application filed in the convention country where the countries are signatories and party to any international or bilateral treaties to which India is also a party to, wherein the same privileges are granted to the citizens of India or the citizens of member nations w.r.t. grant of patent and protection of patent rights; then the priority claimed in the basic application, the priority can be claimed in the complete specification of the patent application filed in the convention country which is termed as convention application.

A convention application shall not be post-dated as mentioned u/s 17(1) to a date later than the date under which provisions of this application has been made. The dating of the patent application means that after the filing of the application & before the grant of patent, which is subject to the provisions of section 9 (which deals with the provisional & complete specification timeline, i.e. within **1 Year** complete specification shall be filed after filing of the provisional application), the controller may after he/she receives the request from the applicant, direct the application to be post-dated to such a date as specified in the request. But no application can be post-dated to no later than **6 Months** from the date on which it was actually made.

But what if in case the multiple priorities are involved when the applicant has filed two or more patent applications in one or more conventions countries wherein those inventions involved in the application constitutes one invention only? Then one application can be made within **12 Months** from the date on which the *earliest* of the application was made.

Under Section 138(1) that deals with the provisions of the convention application, and u/r 121, the period within which the copies of the specification or other documents that can be submitted by the applicant from the date of the receipt of the notice or communication of the controller would be **3 Months.**

There is another route for the filing of the International Application as discussed in the previous book, and that is via PCT route.

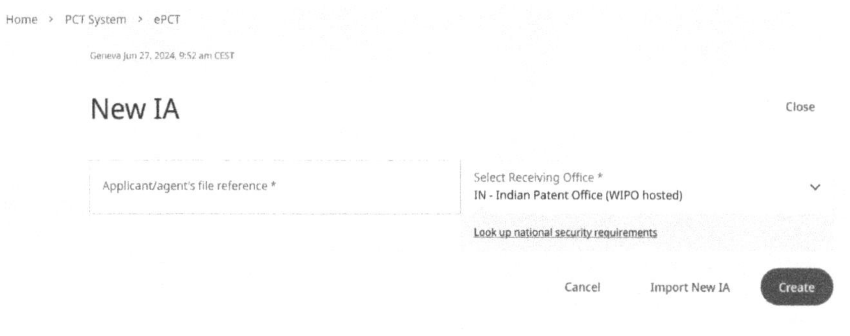

https://pct.wipo.int/ePCTFiling/pages/workbench/newIA.xhtml

In India, the Delhi branch of the Patent Application is the **appropriate office** i.e. the receiving office, the designated office and the elected office concerned, and as being considered as the appropriate office; for dealing with the International Bureau, ISA & IPEA. An international application shall be filed either in Hindi or English language.

In short the timeline would be:

> ➢ *File National Phase Application (eg. in India)*

> ➢ *File PCT within **12 Months***

> ➢ *Within **16 Months** transmittal of ISR (International Search Report)*

> ➢ *Application Published within **18 Months** along with ISR & Written Opinion*

> ➢ *Applicant files for IPRP (International Preliminary Examination Report) at IPEA (International Preliminary Examination Authority), which is Optional from the date of **22 Months** from Priority / OR / Optional International Preliminary Search (SISR)*

> ➢ *Within **28 Months** IPRP / SISR is transmitted to the Applicant*

> ➢ *National Phase Entry within **30-31 Months***

> ➢ *National Phase PCT Filing*

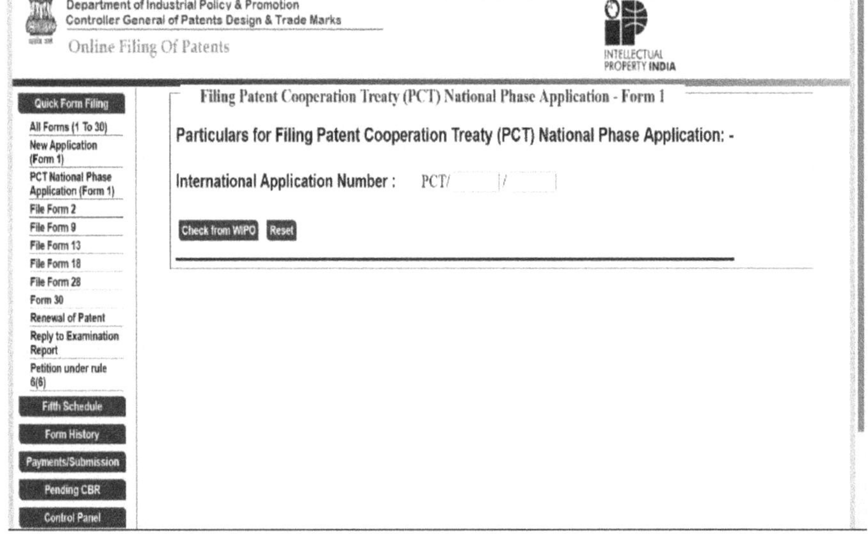

National Phase Entry

Now,

In detail the timeline would be:

*Within **1 Year** of filing of the basic application, file the PCT application.*

*The International filing fee should be paid by the Applicant within a period of **1 Month** from the date of the receipt of the International application.*

*The transmittal fee shall be paid within the period of **1 Month** to the receiving office by the applicant for transmitting of the application to the IB and ISA (R.14.1(c) of Regulations under PCT).*

*Under Article 21(2)(a), the International Application shall be published after the expiration period of **18 Months** from the date of the priority.*

*Within a period of **30/31 Months** the applicant needs to furnish the International Application to the Designated Offices from the priority date and pay the national fees accordingly.*

*Under the Article 7(2)(ii) of the PCT, the designated office may require the Applicant to file such drawings and that should be filed in no case shorter than a period of **2 Months** from the date of the invitation received by the Applicant for filing of the drawings or additional drawings.*

*Priority period would be **12 Months** from the date of filing of the earlier application (R. 2.4 PCT Regulations).*

The appropriate office as mentioned above keeps one copy as the home copy.

The appropriate office transmits a record copy to the International Bureau.

The appropriate office transmits a search copy to the competent ISA.

If the record copy is not received by the International Bureau within the prescribed period of time, then the International Application shall be considered as withdrawn.

*The receiving office shall transmit a record copy to the International Bureau by expiration of **13ᵗʰ Month** from the date of priority. (Rule 22.1 of PCT). And if the IB isn't in the possession of the record copy by the expiration of **14ᵗʰ Month**, but has only received a notification that was sent to the applicant about the international application number & filing date by receiving office; it notifies the applicant and the receiving office, and if within **3 Months** it hasn't been received, then the international application shall be treated as withdrawn under Article 12(3) of PCT, & Rule 22.3 of PCT Regulation. Whereas, defects under Article 11 (1) shall be remedied within the period of **2 Months** by the Applicant u/r 20.7, and after receiving of the same, it shall accord the international filing date only.*

The receiving office shall needs to check whether the International Application contains any defects which may include viz. whether it's not signed or does not contain the prescribed indication concerning the application or does not contain title of the application or does not contain abstract or does not comply to the extent provided in the regulation as mentioned in Article 14(1)(a), and if it contains any defects, then preferably within **1 Month** from the date of the receipt of the International Application, it will have to invite the applicant to correct such defects u/r 26.1 and give the applicant the opportunity u/r 26.2 to make observations within **2 Months** from the date of the invitation. And under Article14(4), the application would be treated as withdrawn if within **4 Months** requirements are not complied with under Article 11(1) items (i) to (iii) which deals with the nationality, residence, right to file IA, language, details of contracting designate state etc.

On request made by the applicant, the appropriate office prepares a certified priority document for seeking priority and transmits it to IB & also to Patent Office, Delhi.

The (Indian) ISA performs the search and prepares the search report. The ISA can be a national office or an intergovernmental office.

The searching authority notifies IB and the applicant about the receipt of the search copy

The searching authority upon receiving the search copy, refers the international application for preparing the international search report ordinarily within a period of **1 Month** but not exceeding **2 Months** from the date of such reference. (R. 19B (2) of Patents Rules)

If the search authority considers that any international application is not complying with the unity of the invention, in accordance with Rule 13 of the regulations of the treaty, then it would send a notice to the applicant & invite the applicant to:

To pay additional fees within **1 Month**

To pay wherever applicable, the protest fee, within **1 Month**

| (Rule 19B (5) of Patents Rules)

The search authority would establish the international search report

If any applicant has paid a protest fees under the protest accompanied by the reasoned statement, then the examination of the protest would be carried by the review committee constituted by the controller

And if not, accordingly, either the total or partial reimbursement of the additional fee would be ordered

*The ISA (international search authority) would establish the ISR (international search report) and the written opinion within the period of **3 Months** from the date of report of the search copy by the searching authority or within the period of **9 Months** from the date of the priority, whichever expires later. Also, Article 17(2)(a), Rule 42 of the PCT Regulation about the time limit and the ISA.*

ISA transmits one copy of the ISR and one copy of the written opinion, both to the IB & to the Applicant (Rule 19D of the Patents Rule). Also, Rule 44 of the PCT Regulations on the same day.

*The Supplementary International Search can also be opted within a period of **22 Months** from the date of priority to be carried out by ISA*

*The search fee shall be paid within a period of **1 Month** to the IB by the Applicant*

*Within a period of **28 Months** from the date of priority, establish the supplementary international search report (SISR), and the authority shall transmit the **same day** to the applicant and to the IB*

*The IB wouldn't transmit to the authority for search above, before **17 Months** from the date of priority or unless the ISR has been generated.*

*Also, the IPEA (International Preliminary Examination Authority) would establish IPRP (International Preliminary Examination Report) with respect of **demand** filed by nationals or residents of a contracting state. This demand would be separate from the IA filed. (Article 31).*

*The Demand can be made within **3 Months** from the date of transmittal to the applicant of ISR or declaration referred to in Article 17(2)(a); or, within **22 Months** from the date of priority. (Rule 54bis of PCT Regulations)*

*The handling fee for the demand made for the benefit of the International Bureau to be collected by the IPEA to which the demand is submitted shall be paid within a period of **1 Month** from the date on which the demand was submitted or **22 Months** from the date of the priority, whichever expires later, under rule 57.3. But the amount shall be refunded if the demand has been withdrawn, if the demand has been sent by that authority to the IB or the demand is considered to have not been submitted only u/r 54.4 or 54bis.1(b). The IPEA may also ask for a preliminary examination fee for its own benefit which has to be submitted as stated above.*

*The IPRP should ordinarily be prepared within the period of **3 Months** but not exceeding **4 Months** from the date of such reference (Rule 19-K of Patents Rules)*

*The period of the IPRP & its transmission should be **28 Months** from the date of the priority; or; **6 Months** from the period specified u/r 69.1 of the regulations under the treaty; or; **6 Months** from the date of receipt by Examination Authority of translation furnished u/r 55.2 of the regulations under treaty, whichever expires last. (Rule(19-L) of the Patents Rules). Also Rule 69.2 of the PCT Regulations.*

*The processing of an international application designating India would not commence before the expiration period of **31 Months** from the date of the priority i.e. the filing date of the application whose priority is claimed, and when there are several priority claims, then the filing date of the **earliest** application whose priority is so claimed. But if an expedited examination is requested by the applicant, then the application would be processed & examined **before 31 Months.***

*Unless, the priority document has been submitted along with the International Application, the filing of the priority document shall be made within the time period of no later than **16 Months** after the priority date. Or as per Rule 21 of the Patent Rules, within **31 Months.** And would further invite the applicant to file if not filed, within the period of **3 Months** or the priority would be disregarded*

*If Amendments are being made under Article 19 of the PCT in the International Bureau, then those amendments need to be made u/r 46.1 of the regulation of pct, and within **2 Months** from the date of transmittal of the international search report to the IB (International Bureau) & to the applicant by the ISA; or, within **16 Months** from the date of the priority date whichever time limit expires later. The amendments shall be filed directly with the International Bureau.*

*If the Amendments are being made under Article 28 of the PCT before the Designated Offices, and if any designated state wherein the examination or processing starts without special request, then the Applicant can within a period of **1 Month** exercise the right from the fulfilment of the requirement under Article 22 of the PCT which states that furnishing a copy of the international application, its translation & the national fee no later than the expiration period of **30/31 Months** from the date of priority; provided that if the communication under Rule 47.1 (which deals with communication to designated offices) has not been effected by the expiration of the time limit* *applicable under Article 22 (which deals with copy, translation, fees, to designated offices) the applicant can exercise no later than **4 Months** after such expiration date.*

*If the Amendments are being made before the Elected Offices under Article 41 of the PCT, then that can be done within **1 Month** from the fulfilment of the requirement under Article 39(1)(a), provided further that if the transmittal of IPRP hasn't taken place as applicable under Article 39, then the applicant can exercise the right no later than **4 Months** after such expiration date.*

*The important thing is the computation of the time limits as from when the time limits should be started. Now, when period are mentioned in years, let's say 1 Year or a certain number of years, then that period would **start on the day following the day on which the relevant event occurred**, and would **end or expire in the relevant subsequent year in the month having the same name and on the day having the same number as the month and the day on which the said event occurred** (as per Rule 80.1 of the PCT)*

*If such period as mentioned above is mentioned in the month, then, the calculation or computation would start, again, **following the day on which the relevant event has occurred and would end or expire subsequent month on the day which has the same number as the day on which the said event occurred.** The same would be applicable if the time limits are expressed in days. **But in case the said time period is expiring on a non-working day or on an official holiday, then the expiration date would be the subsequent day.***

Trademarks Timeline

The filing of the trademarks or what constitutes a trademark, who can file it, when & where from the Indian perspective has been discussed in the earlier book *IP for Everyone, Ethics, Filing, Dilemmas, From An Indian Perspective,* in the most simplest form of language that anyone can read, not only the basics of the entire life cycle of Intellectual Property Rights, but also can initiate the filing procedures by themselves whilst at the same time understanding the most essential, important & day-to-day use of the IPR matters, even at the prosecution level; as not every day, and not every case involves, the interpretation of the law or the statutes itself.

This book covers the timelines involved in different life-cycles of trademark, which covers navigating and protecting one's own intellectual property rights.

Filing of the Trademark

As soon as the trademark application is filed, few timelines should be remembered.

As mentioned in our earlier book, one can even file trademark applications by themselves, but if in case it is filed through an agent or attorney, and further, if due to some (un)foreseen circumstances, such agent or attorney withdraws from the proceedings or authorization, and wherein no principal place of address is mentioned in India; then within a period of **2 Months** from the date of such withdrawal, the applicant or the opponent shall provide the address for service in India; and if not, then such application or opposition is deemed to have been abandoned by the applicant or opponent. And in case of revocation of the authorization by the applicant or opponent wherein no principal place of business is mentioned in India, then in that scenario too, within the period of **2 Months** the applicant or the opponent shall provide the address for service in India, from the date of such revocation, and if it is not provided, then again, such application or opposition is deemed to have been abandoned by the applicant or the opponent.

The trademark application filed shall contain the legible representation of the trademark. What can be filed as a trademark, had already been discussed. But in case, of the 3-D mark, if the registrar is of the opinion that the application does not sufficiently discloses the 3-D mark, then within **2 Months** and upto five different views of the trademark needs to be filed, if the registrar calls upon the applicant to furnish so.

And wherein the application filed is of sound, then the reproduction of it shall contain a recording of not exceeding **30 Seconds**, accompanied with a graphical notation of it in the representation.

Wherein the requirements with respect to the fees has not been properly met as per u/r 10 (2), then to remedy such deficiency, the registrar may ask the applicant to do the same within a period of **1 Month** from the date of such notice, else the application would be treated as abandoned.

The application is examined, and if the registrar thinks the application needs to be modified or amended or limited or be restricted to certain conditions or any further documentation is needed to be furnished or there're certain already existing prior applications, then the registrar in the form of an examination report shall send such report to the applicant and the applicant has to reply to that examination report within a period of **1 Month** and if in case the applicant fails to respond, then that application would be treated as Abandoned.

One can upload that reply to the examination report on the login portal of IPINDIA as explained in the previous book.

There's also a provision of the expedited processing of the application. When the application is filed, an application number is generated. After this, the applicant can file for the expedited request, and the application thus would be examined within a period of **3 Months** from the date of submission of the application.

The remaining part of the prosecution as per the guidelines would be processed expeditiously. Now, herein, the registrar also may limit the number of application eligible for expeditiously processing.

If the reply to the examination report is not satisfactory, then a hearing date would be appointed and the mark would be reflected as **OBJECTED** on the IP portal. Most of the objections would be restricted to either Section 9 or Section 11 of the trademarks act, or if any amendments or modifications or submission of any further documents that needs to be made. For example, sometimes, the applicant has cited the ownership as MSME but has not submitted the MSME certificate, in that case, the examiner would instruct the applicant to submit the documents w.r.t. to the identity about the company or the organization.

The Hearing would be conducted by the hearing officer, and accordingly the mark would either be Refused or be asked for further Amendments or be Accepted and Advertised in Journal, and then as mentioned in the previous book, the mark can either be registered without any opposition or be Opposed within **4 Months** from the date of publication of the mark in the trademark journal.

At **the time of the hearing and before the acceptance** of the application, the registrar may send the application for re-examination including research of the application if any prior marks are existing in the registry. This happens, as sometimes, the examination report has been erroneously issued for some other NICE classifications, or, the examination has missed the pre-requisite documentations from the applicant; but this can be done before the acceptance of the application.

The applicant can seek preliminary advice by the registrar as to the distinctive of the registration of the application. Then a purpose of withdrawal, for the purpose of obtaining repayment of any fee on the filing of the application shall be given in writing within a period of **1 Month** from the date of the receipt of communication u/r 33(2).

On many occasions, the help of whether Attorney or an Agent is taken. The difference between the two is, whilst an Attorney is registered with their local Bar Council; whereas, the Agent is the one who has cleared the trademark exam conducted by the Intellectual Property Office or what is better known as (CGPDTM). Thus, just like Patent Agent, a Trademark Agent also has to renew its enrolment fees **Annually** and failing to do so within a period of **3 Months** on which the annual fees is due, the name of the trademark agent would be removed from the register.

Opposition of the Trademarks

*As mentioned in the earlier book, the time of the opposition proceedings would be **4-2-2-2-1**. That is to say that within the period of **4 Months**, the mark should be opposed by any person interested or the person who has the locus standi on the same.*

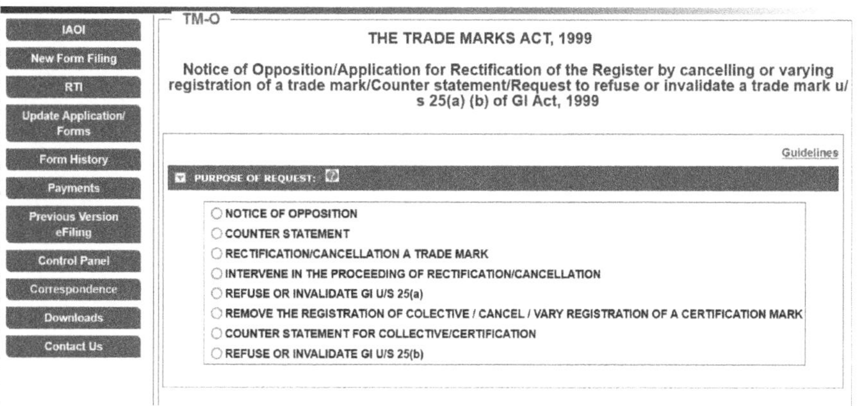

https://ipindiaonline.gov.in/trademarkefiling/newtmForms/frmTM-O.aspx

*The Registrar ordinarily within a period of **3 Months** would serve the notice of opposition to the applicant.*

*Once the Application has been opposed within prescribed period as mentioned above, then, if in case the Applicant wants to further contest the application, he/she can file the Counterstatement within a period of **2 Months** from the date of receipt of the notice of opposition. One thing to be noted in the Counterstatement is that, no Affidavit needs to be filed along with the Counterstatement itself. Only the rebuttal arguments that needs to be made and included in the statements along with the verification part needs to be mentioned at the end of the counterstatement.*

*Once the counterstatement is filed, then the Opponent needs to file the Affidavit in support of the Opposition within a period of **2 Months** from the date of receipt of the counterstatement. One thing to notice from herein henceforth, are both the applicant and the opponent shall deliver the copies of the evidence, affidavits, along with all the exhibits to all the sides, that is, the Tri-Party involved in the proceedings, i.e. Applicant – Registrar of the Trademark -Opponent. Thus, the opponent needs to serve a copy of Affidavit*

& Evidence in support of the opposition along with the exhibits, both to the registrar and to the applicant.

*Within a period of **2 Months** from the receipt of the evidence in support of the opposition filed by the opponent, the applicant should file their evidence in support of the application, along with the cogent exhibits and at the same time serve it to the registrar and to the opponent. One thing to be noted is that **the start date of 2 Months would commence from the date when the applicant has received the evidence from the opponent**. Let us say, the opponent has sent their evidence in support of the opposition on **18/03/2024** or on the online IPINDIA portal it's showing as **18/03/2024**; thus, the applicant is supposed to file their evidence on **18/05/2024**, i.e. within the period of **2 Months**. But let us say, the applicant has received the evidence filed by the opponents on **28/03/2024**, then the **2 Months** would be calculated from the date on which the Applicant has received the evidence filed by the opponents, i.e., from **28/03/2024**, and the last date to file for the evidence in support of the application would be **28/05/2024**, and **NOT**, **18/05/2024**. If the applicant fails to file the evidence in support of the application within the said statutory period, then the application would be considered as abandoned and the opposition would be allowed.*

*Similarly, if the opponents fail to file evidence in support of the opposition within a statutory period of **2 Months**, then that opposition would be deemed to have been dismissed by the opponents for want of prosecution and the application would be proceeded for the registration, and the certificate of the registration would be issued.*

*Next would be if in case the opponents need to file the evidence in reply against the evidence filed by the applicant in support of their application; then within a period of **1 Month** from the date of the receipt of the evidence from the applicant, the opponent would file the evidence in Reply which would be restricted to countering the statements made in the evidence filed by the Applicant.*

Once the above pleading cycle is completed, then no further evidence would be filed by the either side, except taking the leave of the registrar of the trademark. And if the language is other than English or Hindi, then the translation of the same shall be provided by either side both to the registrar and to the opposite side.

Once the pleading stage is completed, then the hearing date would be provided by the registrar to both the sides. It is to be noted that, either party can appear for the hearing or file for Written Statements.

If in case that either of the party neither appears for the hearing nor files written statements, then that matter would be disposed of as an ex-parte decision by the registrar in which case either the application would be treated as abandoned or the opposition would be dismissed as *want of prosecution* and the application would be further proceeded for registration. Provided further that an adjourned request could be filed by either side, and no more than **2 Adjournments** would be given by the Registrar and no **2 Adjournment** would be more than for **30 Days.** The registrar may also ask for the written submissions to be submitted by both parties in support of their arguments made in the hearing along with any case precedence as applicable. The decision of the registrar would be then sent to both the parties as per their addresses on record of service.

Where the application has been made, and subsequently accepted; and wherein notice of opposition has been filed, or, time to file opposition is expired; or the opposition filed has been decided in the favour of the applicant; then the registrar shall register the mark within **18 Months** of filing of application and the trade mark is registered as of the filing date, and that date would be date of registration, and accordingly the certificate of registration would be issued.

But in case the registration of trademark has not been completed due to the default on the part of the applicant within **12 Months**, then the registrar may take appropriate action after giving the notice to the applicant, and if the applicant doesn't fulfil the pending requirements within a specified period of time.

The notice issued u/s 23(3) given to the applicant; shall specify **21 Days** of time from the date thereof, or within a period of time not exceeding **1 Month** if a request is made for the extension of time and with the approval of registrar.

Further, there's a provision of groundless threats of the legal proceedings that the defendant or the person against whom the action has been taken (*the proceedings of infringement*) can counter with; and further could also bring a counter-suit against the plaintiff/petitioner submitting that the threats of infringement and passing-off are unjustifiable; and can also take the injunction against the continuance of such threats, further recover damages as a *person aggrieved* from the person who has brought the infringement suit against the defendant. In such cases, it is not necessary that the person would always be the registered proprietor or the registered user to bring such suits of infringement against the unregistered user only;

as such suits of infringement can also be brought against any different registered proprietor also; thus, the provision of groundless threats can be used by the person aggrieved.

The Status of The Trademark

If the mark is registered from the date of filing of the application, then the validity of the mark would be **10 Years** from the date of its filing. The said mark needs to be renewed, as well as must be in continuous use to keep the mark subsisting and valid.

The application for the renewal can be made not more than **1 Year** before the date of the expiration of the last registration of the trademark. The renewal of the trademark would be made unless the mark has been removed from the register for the non-submission of the renewal fees, or, has been cancelled, or, isn't renewable due to any of the prescribed acts or rules of the trademark, or by the order of any competent court or by the registrar himself/herself. For the renewal, the registrar shall send a notice for the renewal reminding the applicant on the address as mentioned/recorded in the registry, if the renewal has not already been done by the applicant, and that would be sent in not more than **6 Months** before the expiration of the registration of the trademark. Now the applicant must note that the applicant needs to keep its information updated in the Registry/IP offices. Sometimes, when the address for service hasn't been updated, whereas the address of the applicant is changed; then the notice by the registrar for the renewal of the trademark is sent to the old address, which hasn't been updated in the registry; whereas the applicant also forgets to renew the mark; then in that case, the mark is removed from the register and this is then published in the register, and any other person is then eligible to take the mark if applied for the application of the registration of the same or similar mark. If in case the fee with *surcharge* has been paid within the period of **6 Months** from the expiration of the last registration of the trademark, the registrar shall not remove the trademark and shall renew the trademark for a period of **10 Years**.

Now, if a trademark is removed from the register specifically for the non-payment of the fees, then after **6 Months** and within a period of **1 Year** from the expiration of the last registration of the trademark, the registrar can *restore* the mark, if the payment and request for the application has been made in the prescribed form, and further if, the registrar thinks that it's just to do so, then he/she would *restore* the mark, and if required, with certain conditions and limitations, for a further period of **10 Years** from the date of the expiration of the last registration.

There're some conditions involved with respect to the use/non-use of the trademark. For instance, no application of the trademark should be refused nor shall be the permission of such trademark be withheld, on the grounds that the applicant does not intend to use the trademark merely for the reason, and if the registrar is satisfied, that:

> ➤ *the company is about to be formed and that the applicant intends to assign the trademark to that company with a view to use thereof, in relation to the goods & services under which the company operates;*

> ➤ *after the registration of the trademark, the proprietor intends that the trademark is used by a person registered as Registered User.*

And wherein, when the intention to assign trademark to the company as stated above is involved, and a period of not more than **6 Months** is expired; as the Registrar may allow, the company, on an application being made; and then the company is registered as the proprietor of the trademark with respect of the goods or services.

On the other hand, the limitation on the trademark can be imposed on the ground of non-use, or, the trademark can also be removed from the register for the same reason; if it has been proven that the trademark was registered without any bonafide intention of use on the part of the applicant; or, upto a period of **3 Months** before the date of filing of new application, a continuous period of **5 Years** from the date on which the trademark was actually entered in the register or longer, has elapsed during which the trademark was registered, and during which there was no bonafide use; the registered trademark may be taken off, subject to certain conditions. The said trademark may also be permitted to another applicant u/s 12 or if the hon'ble court or registrar as and when think fit to do so.

If the application consists of series application, as discussed in the previous book, at **any time** before the publication of the application in the journal, the applicant may request the division into separate application or applications, and if the registrar is satisfied and after the payment of entire fees and filing of the prescribed documentations, the registrar will divide the application(s) accordingly.

Now, as discussed in the previous book, a registered user can also be registered, in case the registered proprietor & the proposed registered user jointly file in writing to the registrar, along with an agreement authenticated, affidavit of the registered proprietor, giving particulars to the relationship between them, including the degree of the control of the proprietor of the permitted use which their relationship will confer, terms of the agreements, and the restrictions on the permitted use; and if the registered user is registered, then the registrar as and when and how, and during the continuance of the name of register user in the register can call for the information from the registered proprietor to confirm to him within a period of **1 Month** that the agreement filed u/s 49(1)(a) of the trademarks act, at the time of the registration of the registered user, was in fact, in continuance to be in force.

An application for the registration as the registered user has to be filed within a period of **6 Months** from the date of the agreement, else the application itself won't be entertained.

And if in case the registered proprietor fails to notify to the registrar about the same within a prescribed period, then the registered user would cease to exist in the register and would also be notified by the registrar, immediately after the expiry of the said period.

If a notice has been issued wr.t. u/s 50 of the trademarks act, which deals with the variation or cancellation of registration as the registered user, then the notice needs to be sent to all parties, i.e. to the registered proprietor, registered user(s). And if any person intends to intervene in the proceedings, he/she shall within a period of **1 Month** from the receipt of such notification, along with the grounds and statements, would give notice to the registrar about the reason of his/her intervention.

Rectification

The registrar can rectify the register on its own motion. The registrar shall send the grounds, why it has been proposed to rectify the register. The notification shall be sent to the registered proprietor, registered user(s) and to any other person who has an interest in the trademark at that particular period of time, and specify the time which shall not be less than **1 Month** within which any application for hearing can be made by the applicant.

Whilst, the communication after the registration of the registered user shall be sent to the registered proprietor, registered user, interested parties and also to the other registered users; and that name shall be inserted within a period of **3 Months**.

In certain cases, the central government by their notification can ask that the origin of certain goods which are made or produced beyond the borders of India, or, which are made or produced within the borders of India; to indicate the origin and address of manufacturers, or, the person for whom the goods were manufactured, not less than within a period of **3 Months** from the date of such notification.

Condonation of Delay / Extension of Time

U/r 109 of the Trademarks Act, if an application is made for the extension of time u/s 131, in addition to the maximum time that has already been prescribed, then the registrar can extend time not exceeding **1 Month.**

And if in case any person has applied for the discretionary powers of registrar, and seeks hearing; then that person shall inform the registrar within a period of **1 Month** of his intention to be heard. And the registrar shall appoint a hearing date no less than **21 Days**.

There're instances wherein the delay has been condoned by the registry or by the courts on the grounds of natural justice, as the matter should be decided on the merits too. Also, after the amendments in 2017, **the timelines became more *mandatory* than *directory*** i.e. there's no provision to extend the time for filing of any document, other than, what is already mentioned in the acts and rules.

Such timeline starts, let's say in case of filing of the counterstatement or evidence in support of opposition/application, when the party receives the same from registrar/opponent/applicant. And from that date of receipt of receiving of documents, the timeline commences to file counterstatement/ affidavits in support of opposition/application/reply. For example, as mentioned above in the case of **4-2-2-2-1**.

Take this example. The notice of opposition needs to be sent by the registrar to the applicant, and as it is done electronically these days, if in case, the applicant hasn't received the notice of opposition, or the opponent hasn't received the counterstatement sent by the registrar to further file the evidence in support of the opposition; then the applicant or the opponent needs to file an affidavit for non-receiving of concerned documents & further producing *login correspondence details* of the registry logins, from where the applicant/opponent or their attorneys/agents file documents i.e. on IPINDIA login portal.

The same is applicable for filing of the evidence. From the date of receipt of the evidence received by the applicant or opponent from the other side; that date would be the start date to file the evidence in support of application or evidence in support of opposition or evidence in reply, and should be filed within a period of **2 Months**; or **1 Month** in case of the Reply to the Evidence filed by the applicant, as explained above; and further should be served to the other side and also to the registrar.

An example:

Let us say, the Opponent has filed its evidence on **01/01/2024** with the registry, and it's also reflecting on the trademark's registry portal. Now somehow, the opponent sent the evidence to the applicant, as required by him/her to be sent to the applicant under rule 45(1), on **20/01/2024**. The applicant receives the evidence on **24/01/2024** along with the exhibits filed by the opponent. Thus, the applicant's date of filing of the evidence in support of the application commences from **24/01/2024** and it has to be filed within a period of **2 Months** i.e. on or before **24/03/2024**, in the registry and the same shall be served to the opponent as well.

Now, let us say that the Applicant filed the evidence u/r 46 (1) on **22/02/2024** in the registry, but sent the evidence to the Opponent on **20/03/2024** and the opponent received it on **25/03/2024**; then the filing date of **1 Month** u/r 47 of the Reply Evidence by the Opponent, would start from **25/03/2024**, and not from **22/02/2024** when the applicant filed the evidence with the registrar; and the evidence in reply has to be filed on or before **25/04/2024** by the opponent, and also needs to served to the applicant and also to the registrar.

Thus, the receipt when the either party receives the affidavit is more important than the date it was filed with the registry.

In the present times, sending the evidences via email is a common practice; but then the opposite party contending of not receiving the same, could also become an issue, and further as the hearing w.r.t. it may be conducted after years u/r 45(2) or u/r 46(2), of either Applicant's Evidence or Opponent's Evidence being TIME BARRED. Thus, in such a situation, it is always recommended to send the Evidence filed in support of Opposition or Application via Post also, and keep the track receipt in record, so that if in case the opposite party contends of not receiving the email; then at least the postal receipt would corroborate the time details of filing/sending of the evidence u/r 45(1) or 46(1).

Whilst when notices are sent u/s 21(2) & (3), the registrar will send the copy of the notice of opposition or counterstatement, to the applicant or to the opponent. It is sent electronically, both on the correspondence login on the IP portal, as well as on the email. Thus, if in case of not receiving on the email and on the correspondence login as well, then either the applicant or the opponent, at the time of the TIME BARRED hearing, *may* file an affidavit contending the same, along with the screenshots of the correspondence login details and email screenshots as well, proving of not receiving the said notices for filing of the counterstatement u/r 44, or, evidence in support of opposition u/r 45; the condonation of delay *might* be allowed at the time of hearing.

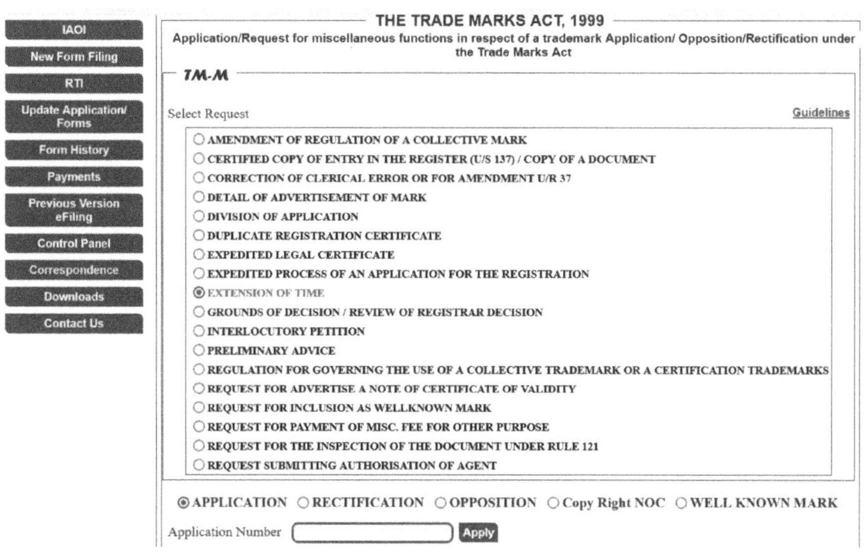

https://ipindiaonline.gov.in/trademarkefiling/newtmForms/frmTM-M.aspx

Copyright VS Trademark

As discussed in the previous book, under Section 45(1) of the Copyrights Act, one needs to request the registrar of trademarks to search for the issuance of certificate that no trademark identical or deceptively similar to the artistic work, which is sought to be registered under the copyright act, has been registered as the trademark under the trademarks act, in the name of any other applicant, other than the applicant. The Certificate is ordinarily issued within **30 Days** from the date of the request made; subject to if the registrar calls upon to the applicant for statement of requirements, then within **2 Months** the applicant needs to comply with it, or the request would be treated as abandoned.

The registrar may also issue a certificate within a period of **7 Working Days** if requested for the expediated issuance of the certificate, and if fees for the same has been paid by the applicant. But an opportunity of hearing would be given if in case of any adverse decision or otherwise.

Rectification Proceedings

In the above section, it has been discussed how and why the trademark can be removed from the register, on the grounds of non-use. The rectification proceedings can also be initiated under Section 47, 57, 68 or 77 of the trademarks act.

S. 47 (basically on the grounds of non-use);

S. 57 (basically on the grounds of absence or omission of any data in the register or any entry wrongly remaining in the register or any entry made without any sufficient cause or anything remining in the register by defect or error);

S. 68 (basically w.r.t. collective marks, for the reason that the mark has been used by the proprietor or the authorized user to mislead the public at large or the proprietor has used the mark contrary to regulations governing the use of mark);

S. 77 (basically w.r.t. the certification mark on the grounds that the registered proprietor is no longer competent enough to use the said mark or has failed to observe the provisions of regulations of its part or the certification mark is no longer advantage for the public at large)

The application for the rectification has to be made by the applicant along with statement of facts; filed at the registry. If in case the registered users are involved, then the copies of the statement be made considering the number of users as well.

*Within **1 Month** the registrar is going to forward the copy of rectification to the registered proprietor and to each registered user and to all those people who've an interest in the application or the registration.*

*Within a period of **2 Months** from the receipt by the registered proprietor of such copy, and within such period not further exceeding **1 Month**, the registered proprietor shall send the counterstatement along with the* *statement, and the registrar shall within a period of **1 Month** serve the same to the applicant making this rectification proceedings. And in case no counterstatement has been filed within the period of **3 Months** from the date of receipt of the application, the applicant of rectification would file the evidence in support of the application under the provision of u/r 45(1), as also discussed above in case of opposition proceedings.*

Then the proceedings u/r from 46-51 shall be applied as mutatis - mutandis to the further proceedings. Any third party other than the registered proprietor, may file for leave to intervene, and the registrar may refuse or allow the said person.

The registrar may also rectify the register on his own motion, u/s 57(4) of the trademarks act. But such notice needs to be sent to all parties concerned including the registered users, registered proprietors, etc. and would specify the time for the hearing that should not be less than **1 Month** from the date of such notice been served for the rectification suo-motu.

The registered proprietor may also apply for the alteration of the trademark, not substantially affecting its identity thereof, and the registrar may refuse or grant such leave, or with the limitations as he may deem fit.

In case of the procedure of the invalidity of the registration pleaded by the accused, as it has been seen u/s 103 & u/s 104 or u/s/ 105 and the accused has been charged under the same, and if further the accused pleads that the registration of trademark is invalid; then, if further the court is satisfied that such defense is prima facie tenable, it shall not proceed with the charge and shall adjourn the matter for a period of **3 Months** from the date on which the plea of the accused is recorded to enable the accused to file the application for rectification against the said trademark before the court on the ground that the registration of the trademark is invalid. And if within the said period of time the rectification proceedings have been initiated by the accused, then against the accused the proceedings in prosecution shall stand stayed, till rectification proceedings have been disposed of. And if in case the rectification proceedings within the said period of time haven't been filed by the accused, then the proceedings against him/her would be initiated as if the registration was a valid registration. The time herein to file the rectification proceedings can be extended also by the court if it deem fit.

International Filing

In the convention application system, a certificate by the registrar of priority needs to be filed along with the application by the applicant if seeking the priority of the convention country. If there're multiple priorities, then the earliest priority would be considered. Usually such certificate to claim the priority is filed along with the application itself, but if in case, that hasn't been filed, then within **2 Months** needs to be filed (R. 24(2) of Trademark Rules). Such a priority is not extendable for the goods or services that are not covered in the convention application.

In case of the international application in which India is the country of origin, the registrar shall after inspecting the documents strictly, forward the verified and certified copies to the International Bureau within a period of **2 Months** from the date of the said application. And when the application falls short of the specified requirements, then instead of forwarding it to the International Bureau, the registrar shall forward it to the applicant, and only after the requirements are met, the registrar shall forward it to the International Bureau (IB) within a period specified in the notice. There's a handling fee for the certification, verification and transmittal of the application by the registrar of the trademark, and such handling fee shall be paid to the registrar in the Indian rupees electronically and online on the ipindia portal by the applicant.

https://efiling.madrid.wipo.int/iwa/air/efiling?execution=e1s1

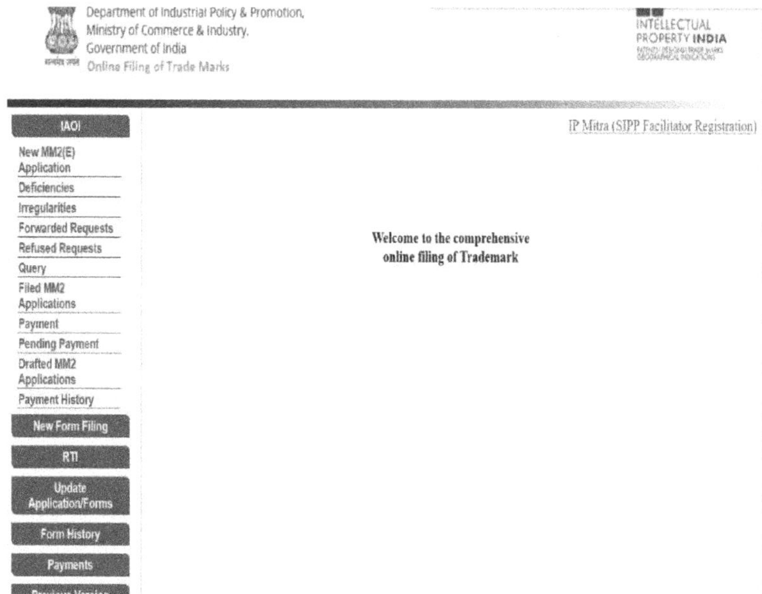

https://ipindiaonline.gov.in/trademarkefiling/user.aspx for filing of the MM2(E) Application

Whereas, the International registration designating India would be kept in the record and any change in International Bureau would be recorded in the same record as well.

The dependency of the International Registration would be **5 Years** on the national basic application or registration, then it would become independent. Means, whether the application has been made u/s 18 of the trademarks act, or, u/s 23 has been withdrawn, or cancelled, or, refused, or transferred, or assigned, or the protection of the goods has been restricted or removed, or, expired; then that would affect the protection resulting from such International Registration for a period of **5 Years**, and would cease to have effect thereafter. But in case an action is taken against the said decisions before the expiry of **5 Years** of an international registration, then any final decision resulting in the above scenarios shall be deemed to have taken place before the expiry of **5 Years**.

Subject to the registrar has to transmit all such information to the International Bureau during the period of **5 Years.**

Wherein the International Registration (IR) in which India is designated, and after receipt of an advice from the International Bureau, and after keeping such record, shall be examined within a period of **2 Months** from the date of such receipt (Rule 69 of trademarks act); and where there's no ground of refusal to grant protection, then the registrar would advertise the mark in the trademark journal within **6 Months** from the date of receipt of advice (Rule 69 (3) of trademark rules)

And any office would notify its refusal within the period of **18 Months** (Article 5(2)(b) of the Madrid Protocol) from the date on which such advice was received; or, after hearing of the application, registrar can grant the protection with limitations, or, may not grant at all, or, with some additional or different conditions; after the registrar is satisfied to do so; and inform the International Bureau within the said period of time. And when the registrar finds nothing on the particulars as shared that would've lead to refuse of the grant of protection; then within the specific period, advertise the international registration.

And if within a period of **18 Months** no opposition has been received, or, the time to file the opposition has been expired; then the registrar within the above period of time from the date of receipt of advice received from the IB, notify the IB about the acceptance of extension of the protection. And in case the registrar fails to do so within the specified period of time, then it shall be deemed to have been accepted the extension of protection of the trademark.

And let us say the protection has not been extended, then the holder of the international registration would've the same remedy as any other person to initiate further action.

Further, as stated earlier, the changes in the basic registration or application would affect the international registration for the period of **5 Years;** and so as for the protection of the designated applications as well.

And as mentioned about the lifeline of the trademark, the international registration would be effective and valid for a period of **10 Years** and needs to be renewed every **10 Years** to keep it valid and subsisting. And further, a grace period of **6 Months** would be allowed for renewal of the international registration, subject to the payment of surcharge fees, as stated in the above paras (Article 7(4) of the Madrid Protocol); but before **6 Months** from the date of the expiry of the international registration, IB would send an unofficial notice of reminder to renew the registration.

Wherever the International Application complies of all the basic requirements, wherein India is the country of origin, then the registrar within a period of **2 Months** forward the same to the International

Bureau from the receipt of the said application. And as stated above, if the International Application doesn't meet the requirements, then the registrar shall first forward it to the applicant for the correction of the defects and only after the defects are being remedied, registrar shall forward it to the International Bureau.

And where the opposition has been filed, then registrar shall inform the IB about the provisional refusal, and further the opposition would be further proceeded in accordance to the provisions of u/r 42 to 51 as *mutatis mutandis*, as already been explained in the above sections of the opposition proceedings.

And where the protection of trademark designating India is for the collective or certification marks, then the regulation governing the use of such trademarks would be submitted directly by the holder of IR to the registrar within a period of **1 Month** from the date of the advice by the IB as mentioned above.

The convention application is already discussed and also the International Filings filed via the Madrid Protocol in any of the contracting party. But there're certain timelines that needs to be aware of:

A basic application or the basic registration needs to exist in the country of origin.

*A person can file for the protection of its trademark globally via Madrid Protocol route, with a priority of not more than **6 Months** (timeline as fixed under **Article 4** of the Paris Convention) at the country of origin. Note, that for the Patents, the international priority is **12 Months** and for the trademarks and industrial designs, it is **6 Months** each.*

However, in some contracting parties, one needs to show the intention for use of the trademark therein. Like for example, in the US, along with the MM2 Form, one needs to also add MM18 Form as declaration to use the trademark in the said country.

In any of the International Application, one needs to indicate both the nationality of the applicant and legal status, if in case the company is a legal entity.

The international application would contain the details & particulars that's been presented in the basic application or registration. And the office of origin shall certify that particulars, before sending it to the International Bureau; including the mark whether it's B&W or Color etc.

*The International Bureau shall register the application and the international registration shall bear the **same date** as date on which the international application was being made, provided that the International Application has been received by the International Bureau within a period of **2 Months** from that date. And if not received, then the international registration shall bear the date on which the application was received by the International Bureau.*

Once it has been registered, the date of the protection of the mark would be same as if filed at any other contracting party office. And the indication of goods in the application shall not bind on the contracting parties.

*If the IB considers that there's an irregularity in the IA (International Application), it shall notify the applicant, and also inform the office of origin, and within a period of **3 Months,** such irregularities may be remedied by the applicant from the date of such notification. And if it is not remedied, then the International Application is considered as deemed to be abandoned, and it would be intimated by the IB to both the office of origin and to the applicant.*

*As mentioned, some contracting parties require to file declaration of intention to use the mark within that territory; thus, if such part is missing in the application, and if the IB has notified the same, then within a period **2 Months** the applicant has to file the declaration*

*Wherein the IB considers that fees paid related to the application is less than prescribed, then it can notify to the office of origin and to the applicant, and then either of them can pay the fees within **3 Months** from the date of such notification, and if the fees is not paid, then the application would be considered as abandoned and the decision would be notified to both the office of origin and to the applicant (Rule 11 (3) of the Madrid Regulation).*

*Basically, similar irregularities can be corrected either by the applicant or by the office of origin within a period of **3 Months** from the date of such notification by the IB (RULE 11 of the Regulation)*

If the irregularities are found to be w.r.t. classification of goods or services, then as per the requirement of rule 9(4)(a)(xiii), the IB shall make a proposal of its own and shall send the same to the office of origin and to the applicant as well.

*The office of origin can send an opinion differing from the proposal to the IB within a period of **3 Months** and if in case within the period of **2 Months** the IB doesn't receive neither the proposal of the office of origin nor anything from the applicant, then the IB would send a reminder of proposal within* *a period of **2 Months** which would not affect the **3 Months** timeline of the above under which the office of origin needs to send the proposal. (Rule 12 of the Madrid Regulation)*

The IB can also withdraw such proposal sent, or, it can modify the proposal sent, or, can confirm its proposal.

*If the office of origin doesn't send any proposal within a period of **3 Months** as stated above, then if the proposal sent by the IB mentions any amount due to the proposed classification and groupings; then that fees needs to be paid within a period of **4 Months,** else, the international application would be termed as abandoned. And if according to the opinion as sent by the office of origin, is payable within a period of **3 Months** else the international application would be treated as abandoned and the same would be communicated to both the applicant and to the office of origin. And if in case the opinion has been accepted and the IB withdraws its proposal, then no fees would be paid by the applicant.*

*If in case the international application has indicated goods or services that are too vague to be considered under the classification, then the IB shall either substitute the term or may delete the term, and the office of origin may make a proposal remedying the set of goods or services within the period of **3 Months** from the date of such notification from the IB. (Rule 13 of Madrid Regulation)*

When the entire details and particulars in the international application are correct and acceptable at the IB, it would be registered as the International Registration (IR), and it would then send certificate to the holder. The data this registration would include:

➢ *All data included in the International Application filed;*

➢ *The priority claim where the date of the priority claim is not more than **6 Months** before the date of the international registration, means one can claim for the priority of not more than **6 Months** from the date of the international registration;*

➢ *The date and the number of the International Registration.*

Refusals

Now, the information related to possible opposition, & time limit for notifying provisional refusal based on an opposition (*Rule 16 of the Regulations*), wherein it has become apparent that with regard to international registration designating the contracting state/party, that opposition period would expire too late for any provisional refusal based on an opposition, to be notified to the International Bureau within a period of **12/18 Months** time-limit referred to in Article 5(2)(b), it would inform the International Bureau of the number and the name of the holder, of that International Registration. And if the office has informed the International Bureau of the fact that the time limit for filing oppositions will expire within **30 Days** preceding the expiry of the **18 Months** time limit and of the possibility that oppositions may be filed during those **30 Days**, a provisional refusal based on an opposition filed during the said **30 Days** may be notified to the International Bureau within **1 Month** from the date of filing of the opposition (Rule 16 of Madrid Regulations). There're certain kinds of provisional refusals:

> ➢ *Ex-officio Provisional Refusal – grounds on which the protection cannot be granted;*

> ➢ *Provisional Refusal Based on the Opposition – protection cannot be granted due to opposition has been filed;*

> ➢ *Or it can be both.*

Within the period of no less than **2 Months,** the applicant can file *review or appeal or response* petition against either of the ex-officio refusal or the provisional refusal based on the opposition, from the day it was transmitted to the applicant. The said refusal shall indicate all the details wherein it needs to be filed, the review or the appeal or response, within the specified period of time.

The IB shall also register the details of such provisional refusals into the details of the International Register.

The IB shall not consider the provisional refusal, if it doesn't have all the details, i.e., the number of the international registration, the details of the grounds on which the provisional refusal has been issued, or if it has been sent too late to the IB by the contracting party.

The office can also send a notice intimating to the IB that the ex-officio examination has been completed and it has found no grounds for the provisional refusal but the application is still open for the opposition by the third parties, with a date that to which date such oppositions can be filed by the third parties. The IB would've to and as stated above, records all the details and particulars about the status of the international registration into the international register.

Within the period of **18 Months** from the date of the International Registration, such provisional refusal shall be notified by the office to the IB.

There are some short forms that one need to be aware of:

IRDI -> International Application Designating India

IAOI -> International Application Originating India

In case of the IRDI Applications, it would be examined within a period of **2 Months** from the date of the international registration was notified to India and the date of receipt of advice (R. 69 (1) of Trademark Rules). And if there're no grounds of refusal, then within **6 Months** from the date of receipt of advice from the IB, registrar would advertise the particulars of the application in a separate journal. With respect to India, if the holder of the International Registration receives through the IB, a provisional refusal, then the holder of the International Registration would've the same rights and remedies as if the application has been directly filed in India. And as discussed above, the holder of the International Registration can either amend the goods at the IB or limit the scope of the application in accordance with the provisional refusal received. And any such amendments accorded or recorded, at the International Registration also. And if in case the hearing has been scheduled, then it would be conducted as per the provisions of the local laws of the designated party. In case, no response with respect to the provisional refusal is received by the office, then the confirmation of the provisional refusal would be communicated to the IB. Whereas, when the International Registration is accepted in India, then it would be published in the separate journal.

And as discussed in the opposition section, if in case the international registration is accepted, then it would be open for the opposition by any other third party within a period of **4 Months.** And if in case the opposition has been received by the designated office, then it would be disposed off as if any other national application and the provisional refusal based on the opposition would be communicated to the holder of the international registration and further the opposition would be disposed off as per the trademark acts and rules and the decision would be notified to the IB accordingly. In this case, Rule 17, 18, 18bis and 18ter of the Madrid Regulation; Article 4, 5 of the Madrid Protocol; u/s 36E of trademarks act, would be applicable.

Now, here is a tricky timeline, which can be summarized by giving an example of India. Let us say that the international registration has been found to be acceptable and no ground of refusal is accorded, and, the timeline to file the opposition too *hasn't* expired, i.e. **4 Months** from the date of publication in the journal, and the period of **18 Months** after the notification of the IRDI is likely to expire; then as discussed above, a statement would be sent by the designated office about the *ex officio* examination has been completed but the timeline for the opposition of the mark is still opened by the third parties, and the date by which the opposition can be filed.

Two things should be considered; one is provisional refusal and the other thing is provisional refusal confirmed.

And in case the provisional refusal has been withdrawn, then the trademark would be granted protection. And as the mark is already registered at the International Bureau, that's why a certificate of the same would be issued.

The International Registration would be renewed at the International Bureau, from the date on which the renewal fees was due, even if the fees was paid within the grace period of **6 Months** after the due date as discussed.

One important thing to be noted in the Article 5(2)(c) of the Madrid Protocol is that, when the refusal of protection may result from an opposition, then the office may notify a refusal of the protection after a period of **18 Months,** only if:

> ➤ *The designated office has informed the IB that the opposition may be filed after the expiry period of **18 Months;***

> ➤ *The notification of the refusal based on an opposition is made within a time limit of not more than **7 Months** from the date on which the opposition period begins; wherein the notification must be made within a time limit of **1 Month** from the expiry of the opposition period.*

License

When any license has to be recorded, it can be made directly to the IB, or by the contracting party accepting the license itself. If there are some defects or irregularities in it, then it has to be remedied within the period of **3 Months** from the date of the notification of the irregularity by the IB, else, such request shall be Abandoned and the remaining fees would be issued, if paid. And if it has been complied with all the requirements, it will be recorded in the International Registration and shall be notified to the holder of the IR, and to the designated office.

The validity of the mark at IB would be **10 Years** with the possibility of the renewal in recurrence.

And when the period of **5 Years** expires, then that IR becomes independent from the Basic Application or the Basic Registration. And if before the said period, the basic application or basic registration is lapsed or renounced or withdrawn or revoked or cancelled or invalidated with respect to some or all of the goods or even if such proceedings have begun before the period of **5 Years**, then it would affect the IR, provided that if the same application has been transformed into a regional or national application by filing of the same with the same priority as of the IR within the period of **3 Months,** with the same class of goods & services; and fulfilling all the requirements as per the national or regional laws.

Division/Merge

Wherein several applications have been merged into a basic application or a single basic application has been divided into several applications, then the office of origin shall notify to the International Bureau about the same wherein the details would be included as the number of the IR or the Basic Application/Registration; the name of the applicant; and the number of applications that have been divided or merged into a single basic application/registration; mutatis mutandis, as above would apply if that has been done within a period of **5 Years.** (*Rule 23 of the Madrid Regulations*)

If in case the law of any designated contracting party does not allow it to send any communication to the holder of the IR directly, then the designated contracting party can request the IB to directly send the communication to the holder of the IR itself on behalf of it.

Change in Address/Ownership/Amendments

A request for recordal of the ownership, or, change in the address, or, limiting the goods & services with respect to the designated contracting parties, or, renunciation of goods or services, or, change in the name of legal entity, or, cancellation of IR w.r.t. some or the other goods, or, change in the name of the representative.

Either the holder can send the changes or the office of origin or both; and also, in case of signing, either any one of them, or, both of them wherever applicable can sign and send the same to the IB. And if any irregularities are found in the request itself, then it has to be remedied by the holder or the designated contracting party or both.

The said irregularity can be remedied within a period of **3 Months** from the date of such notification. Else the request would be considered as abandoned and would be notified to both the office and the holder, and the part of the refund fees would be issued.

The change shall be recorded in the international register. The change in the ownership can be restricted to some or more designated parties or to some or more goods or services; again, which shall be recorded in the International Register from time to time. In most of the cases, the irregularity has to be remedied within a period of **3 Months** from the date of notification from the International Bureau.

The merger of the International Registrations can also happen if in case the same holder becomes the owner of the two or more of the international registrations. Such request can either be made directly or through the designated office of the contracting party.

The applicant may appoint one or more representative(s) before the International Bureau. And when several representatives are being appointed, then the one mentioned in the first shall be considered as the representative. Again, in case of the irregular appointment, a notice would be sent, either to the office, or to the holder itself, and that needs to be remedied, and if not remedied, then all the information is sent to the holder of the IR, and not to the representative on record. The recordal of such representatives shall be cancelled on the request made by the holder of the application, or, by the representative itself.

If the change in ownership has no effect in the office, let's say in the designated office of India, then within a period of **18 Months** from the date of notification when it was sent by the IB/WIPO, a declaration of the same would be intimated to the IB by the Office.

Take another example. If errors have been corrected by the IB and has been notified to the designated office, then the office can scrutinize the said corrections, and if and when found defects in it, can communicate the refusal of the corrected errors from its side to the IB within the period of **12 Months** from the date of such corrections. And if in case, no refusal has been sent, then the international registration would be updated. Whether its corrections of any error, or change in ownership, or license or otherwise, all such corrections would be scrutinized at the designated office to evaluate whether it is compliable w.r.t. the local laws of the nation.

When IR Becomes National/Regional Before 5 Years

Now, when the International Registration can be transformed into national or regional application? As discussed above, if under the Article 6(4), the international registration has been cancelled at the request of the office of origin, then the holder of the IR can file to the designated office of any of the contracting parties, in the territory wherein the IR has effect, as discussed in the above sections, then the date of that national application would be treated as the date of the international application and if in case it enjoyed the priority, it would also enjoy such priority, subject to the certain conditions:

1. *that such application has to be filed within a period of **3 Months** from the date on which the international registration was cancelled;*
2. *the goods and services shall be same for both of the IR & of the contracting party; and*
3. *further it should be in coherence with the local laws wherein within a period of **3 Months** such application has been filed.*

In both the patents and the trademarks section, we've seen that:

1. *Intent of Using;*
2. *Renewing;*

are the two aspects that are required. And as stated from the Indian perspective also, the trademark can be removed, revoked; so, as patent can be subjected to compulsory license, revocation, on the grounds of non-use and non-renewal.

Whilst for the trademark application in the US via Madrid, the holder of the IR needs to file the *Intent of User Form* along with the application of IR.

And the requirement of the local attorneys/agents come into picture, in case of provisional refusal, and further, in case of the opposition, the holder of the IR wants to defend its rights within the local territory; in the Indian context, provisions of Rule 42-51 shall apply for the same. As the life cycle of the opposition would be:

$$4 \to 2 \to 2 \to 2 \to 1$$

Further, the meaning of the three words needs to be understood in terms of the change in particulars of IR as one of the following restrictions by the holder of IR:

Limitation: of the list of goods that may affect some or all designated parties;

Renunciation: protection with respect of some, but not all, in the designated contracting parties, for all the goods & services;

Cancellation: of the IR with respect to all the designated contracting parties for some or all of the goods and services.

If the above request isn't against the provisions of the designated contracting party's trademark laws, then it would be updated; in India's context, in the IRDI records.

And further we notice, most of the timelines are restricted to **1/2/3/6/12/18 Months.** In any case, the notice would always mention the timeline for filing of any response.

Copyright Timeline

Why copyright is needed, its effects in the modern world, how and why it shall be protected in the age of AI, what is the difference between copyright and patents, or, copyright and designs, or, copyright and trademarks, or copyright and geographical indications, were already discussed in the previous book: *IP For EVERYONE – Part-I* and as mentioned above, in the language, that can be understood by anyone and everyone, irrespective of having any intellectual property rights background or not.

When it comes to the timeline of the copyrights, then one needs to understand that it differs from all the above viz. patents, trademarks, designs, GI; as in case of the copyright, it comes into existence the moment it is materialized i.e. the moment it comes into existence or created. The registration of it again is the prima facie evidence of validity, i.e., just like in the case of trademark, its registration isn't necessary; similarly in the case of copyright also, its registration isn't necessary, but it becomes helpful at the time when any legal dispute arises. But unlike the trademark which has to be kept renewing every **10 Years** , copyright need not to be renewed once it gets registered. There is a *term* of copyright for different entities, as is given below, be an author or artist or broadcasting agency or producer etc. and unlike the trademarks which when not renewed becomes open for the interested person to acquire it under certain circumstances; in the copyright that isn't the case, until the term of the copyright expires which is a very long period of time.

Again, in case of patents, we have Convention Application structure or PCT for the protection of the patent outside the territory of India. In case of trademarks, we have Convention Application system and the Madrid Protocol for protection of trademarks outside the territory of India; but in the case of Copyrights, instead of having such platforms, we have an International Copyright order of the countries who are a part of the Berne Convention, Universal Copyright Convention, WTO, Phonograms Convention, TRIPS etc. and the reciprocal rights in the copyrights that are being protected in the Work that was first made or published or remained unpublished.

The term of the copyright in any work shall not be exceeded which was enjoyed by it in its country of origin.

Before going into the details of the copyrights, the definitions as who is defined as the holder of the copyright, whether in terms of being the original creator, or a licensee, or an assignee, or the owner, or the producer etc. are as herein mentioned below:

Author:

In relation to any literary/dramatic work, author of the work;

In relation to musical, the composer;

In relation to artistic work other than a photograph, the artist;

In relation to a photograph, person taking the photograph;

In relation to cinematographic film or sound recording, the producer;

In relation to any work generated by the computer, the person generating that content;

In relation to the composer of a musical work, person who composes the music;

Copyright society means, society registered under Section 33(3);

Works:

Computer programme;

Engravings include etchings, lithographs, wood-cuts, prints and other similar works, not being photographs;

Literary Work includes computer programmes, table and compilations;

Performance related to the Performer's Rights means any visual & acoustic performance made by the Performer who can be actor, singer, musician, dancer etc.;

Work of sculpture includes casts & models;

In the previous book, we have seen the example of DABUS, as why it wasn't considered as the natural person, as not being human. Further, in the case of the world of ChatGPT, which collects mammoths of data across different domains to produce an output, which might also be a copyright infringement.

Now, just like an Author; Broadcast means communicating to the public by means of wirelessly diffusing it, in one or more forms of sounds, songs & images; or by the wire.

Calendar Year means the year commencing on **1st day of January**.

Assignment

Whenever there is any assignment involved, it shall be in writing and duly verified and signed both by the assignor & the assignee or either of their authorized agents. If not, it shall *not* be considered as Valid; and also, it should specify the amount, royalty or any other consideration in it.

Whereas, if the assignee does not exercise the right assigned within a period of **1 Year** from the date of the assignment, then the assignment would be considered as deemed to be lapsed unless any clause subject to it has been specified in the assignment itself. (S.19(4))

And if in case the period of the assignment is not mentioned, then it shall be **5 Years** from the date of the assignment. (S. 19(5))

And if the territorial limit hasn't been specified in the assignment, then it would be within the territory of India only, and if in case any dispute arises, then no order of revocation can be made within a period of **5 Years** as mentioned above.

This revocation happens when the assignee fails to make sufficient exercise of the rights assigned to him. Also, if any complaint has been received w.r.t. assignment, then the efforts shall be made by the Commercial Courts to pass a final order within a period of **6 Months** from receiving the complaint. (S. 19-A)

Author's Rights & Term

The author of any work as mentioned above can relinquish its work in the copyright (*all or specific part*) by giving notice to the registrar. The registrar would publish it into its official Gazette, and within a period of **14 Days** from the publication of the notice, post this relinquished notice on the official website and would keep that for the period of no less than **3 Years.**

Now, the term of the copyright is almost similar for all, except in few cases it differs. It *isn't* alike **10 Years** + Recurrence until further renewal for another **10 Years** and continued as in case of trademark; **10+5** Years in case of Designs; **20 Years** as in case of Patents, with annual renewal of it; **10 Years** + Recurrence until further renewal for another **10 Years** and continued as in case of Geographical Indication.

Term of the Copyrights would be:

1. For the dramatic, literary, musical or artistic work that is published within the lifetime of the author, it shall be the **lifetime + until 60 Years** from the beginning of the calendar year next **following the year in which the author dies**. (S.22)

2. For anonymous or pseudonymous works: In the case of literary, musical, artistic, or dramatic works (other than a photograph), which is published as stated, it would subsist until **60 Years** from the beginning of the calendar year next following the year in which the work is **first published**; and if the identity of the author is disclosed before the expiry of the said period, then it would be until **60 Years** from the beginning of the calendar year next **following the year in which the author dies**. (S.23)

3. For posthumous works: In case of literary, dramatic or musical work or an engraving, the copyright shall subsist until **60 Years** from the beginning of the calendar year next following the year in which the work is **first published** or, where an adaptation of the work is published in any earlier year, from the beginning of the calendar year next following that year. (S.24)

4. For Cinematographic Films: **60 Years**, from the beginning of the calendar year next following the year in which the film is published. (S.26)

5. For Sound Recording: **60 Years**, from the beginning of the calendar year next following the year in which the sound recording is first published. (S. 27)

6. For Government Works: **60 Years**, from the beginning of the calendar year next following the year in which the work is first published. (S.28)

7. For Public Undertaking: **60 Years**, from the beginning of the calendar year next following the year in which the work is first published. (S.28-A)

8. For International Organizations: If the provisions of **S. 41** applies, then **60 Years**, from the beginning of the calendar year next following the year in which the work is first published. (S.29)

Herein, in copyright also, just alike patents, but unlike trademarks, there is a provision of compulsory licenses. For instance, for the statutory license of cover versions, the person making sound recording shall *not* make until the expiration of **5 Years** after the end of the year in which first sound recording was made. (S. 31-C)

Licenses

For a license to publish or produce translation, one can apply for the same to the Commercial Court after a period of **7 Years** from the first publication of the work.(S.32)

Also, for the literary or dramatic work in any language, other than an Indian work; provided that this can also be done after a period of **3 Years** from the first publication of the work if that is required for the purpose of teaching, scholarship or research. Further, the same application for translation can be made after a period of **1 Year** if such translation is in a language not in general use in the developed country (S. 32(1-A)). These licenses are only granted if the translated work is out of print, or, as mentioned above, **7/3/1 Years** have lapsed and no publication has been made. Furthermore, the applicant has made due effort to contact owner and in case the owner could not be located, the publisher; took not less than **2 Months** before making such application. Whereas, in case of clause 1-A, **6 Months;** and in case of contacting the owner or the publisher, **6 or 9 Months** have elapsed and the owner/publisher haven't published the translated work. (S.32)

There is a license to reproduce and publish works of certain purposes, viz, literary, scientific or artistic work, wherein such works aren't available in India or are out of print for **6 Months**; license could be granted after the relevant period (*i.e.* **7 Years** *in case of the fiction, poetry, drama, music or art from the date of first publication;* **3 Years** *in case of natural science, physical science, mathematics or technology;* **5 Years** *in case of any other work*) is expired for the reproduction or publication of any work; when the copies of such editions are not available in India; or such copies aren't put on sale for a period of **6 Months**; or to the general public at a price reasonably related to that what is charged in India for the same comparable work by the owner of the right of the reproduction, or by any other person authorized by him on his/her behalf. But before that, the applicant has to make sure that he has approached the owner but was denied for the same and would have to prove his own due diligence. Further, a period of **6 Months** has elapsed for the reproduction and publication of any work w.r.t. natural science, physical science, mathematics or technology; or a period of **3 Months** in case of any other work, has elapsed, from the date of making such request to the owner and the owner hasn't published the reproduction work or by the person authorized by the owner within a said period as **6 Months / 3 Months.**

Now, such licenses can be terminated for the following reasons:

1. owner, or publisher authorized by him, publishes a translation in the same language, with the same content & reasonable of the same price; provided that no such termination shall take place before a period of 3 Months.

As discussed, just alike in Patent, a compulsory license can also be granted under the Copyright Act also. And any copyright for the benefit of the disabled on a profit basis can be applied, and such application shall be disposed or endeavor be made to dispose of such application within a period of **2 Months** from the date of receipt of such application received by the Commercial Court.

Copyright Societies

The owner of the copyright work has the right in its individual capacity to grant licenses which shall be in consistence with the obligation, *if any*, as a member of the copyright society.

As far as the literary, dramatic, musical or artistic works are concerned that are incorporated in the cinematographic films, or sound recording, that shall be carried out only through a copyright society duly registered under the copyright acts and rules. (S.33(1))

The Central Government shall not register more than 1 Copyright Society for doing the business in the same class of works.

The registration of the copyright society shall be for a period of **5 Years** and can be renewed, before the said period of time. And if the conduct of the copyright society would be detrimental towards the authors and owners of the copyright; registrar may suspend the registration of the copyright society, pending enquiry for a period of not exceeding **1 Year.**

As we have seen the rights conferred to different individuals and the organizations involved, and also its terms. There is another special right known as broadcasting reproduction rights w.r.t. broadcasts, the term of which shall be until **25 Years** from the beginning of the calendar year next following the year in which broadcast was made. (S. 37).

Besides this, there is another right known as Performer's Right which shall subsist until **50 Years** from the beginning of the calendar year next following the year in which performance was made.

But once a performer by a written agreement consented for incorporation of his performance in the cinematographic film, then he/she shall not object to the enjoyment of the producer's right, until being written anything contrary to it; but would be entitled for the royalties for the *commercial* use. And as discussed in the previous book also, the performer would have the moral rights; means, rights against the distortion or mutilation or modification that has affected the reputation of the performer.

And further as discussed in the previous book, there are certain acts that cannot be considered as an infringement viz. but not limited to, alike, fair dealing of the use of any copyrighted work for the personal or private use, including research, criticism of the work, reporting of the current events and current affairs, for making adaption or the copy of the computer program *only* for the purpose of non-commercial use & personal use or to make a copy of it as a backup, reproduction of any work for the purpose of judicial proceedings; (S. 52(1)(h)) the publication in a collection, mainly composed of non-copyright matter, bona fide intended for instructional use, and so described in the title and in any advertisement issued by or on behalf of the publisher, of short passages from published literary or dramatic works, not themselves published for such use in which copyright subsists: Provided that not more than **2 such passages** from works by the same author are published by the same publisher during any period of **5 Years**.

Any person who infringes knowingly any copyrighted work shall be punishable for a period of **6 Months** which could exceed to **3 Years** and a Fine which shall be not less than **50 Thousand** rupees but may extend to **2 Lac** Rupees. And on the second conviction, it would be not less than **1 Year** and may extend upto **3 Years.**

Appeals

Any person can appeal against the order of the Registrar of the Copyright, within a period of **3 Months** from the date of the order and decision to the Hight Court. And any person aggrieved from order of the magistrate as mentioned above can make an appeal within a period of **30 Days** to the appropriate court.

International Protection of the Copyright

Under Article 5(2) of the Berne Convention, there is a provision of automatic protection and independence of protection of the copyright work as it comes into existence as soon as it is created or materialized. As the article clearly mentions that the enjoyment of these rights shall not be subject of any *formality*. Thus, as soon as the copyright work is created, it is protected globally, not by the formality, but by the global reciprocal treaties.

And such treaties are BERNE, WTO, TRIPS etc. Enjoyment of the copyright shall be independent of the existence of the protection in the country of origin of the work, but the protection of the copyright shall be governed by the laws of the country where the protection is claimed.

Design Timeline

The Design as such has been discussed in the previous book, its comparison, differences with the trademarks, copyrights, patents and G.I.s.

As per section 2(d) of The Design Act: *only the features of shape, configuration, pattern, ornament or composition of lines or colours applied to any article whether in two dimensional or three dimensional or in both forms, by any industrial process or means, whether manual, mechanical or chemical, separate or combined, which in the finished article appeal to and are judged solely by the eye; but does not include any mode or principle of construction or anything which is in substance a mere mechanical device, and does not include any trade mark as defined in clause (v) of sub-section (1) of section 2 of the Trade and Merchandise Marks Act, 1958 (43 of 1958) or property mark as defined in section 479 of the Indian Penal Code (45 of 1860) or any artistic work as defined in clause (c) of section 2 of the Copyright Act, 1957 (14 of 1957).*

Application of the design shall be made within a period of **6 Months** from the date of first exhibiting the design or article or publishing it to any exhibition, which could have invalidated or prevented the design to get registered, due the provision as to the exhibitions, if done later; provided that given previous notice of it to the controller. (S.21 of Design Act).

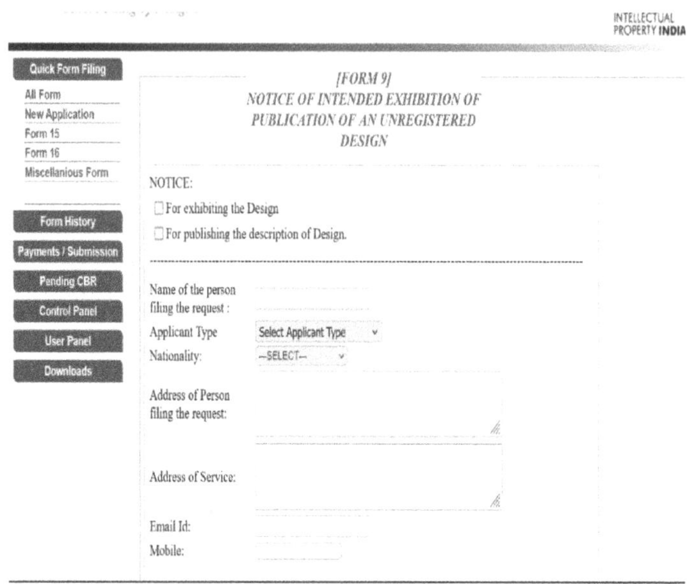

https://online.ipindia.gov.in/eDesign/PATfORMS/desFORM9.aspx

When any person or entity becomes the owner of the design via assignment or transmission or any other operation of law, then such an assignment or mortgage or license has to be filed within a period of **6 Months** from the date of execution of such an instrument, or, within a further period of **6 Months** in aggregate if the controller may allow for the same (S. 30(3)). The registration in the design office is different from the date of execution. Such instruments shall come into effect on the date of execution only, whilst, the date of the registration in the design office would be as and when registered.

Appeal

The appeal from the order of the controller shall be made to the High Court within a period of **3 Months** from the date on which the receipt of the certified order has been received by the applicant. (S.36 of the Design Act)

As there is NICE classification in trademarks, similarly, there is LOCARNO classification as per the edition of the International Classification for the Industrial Design (LOCARNO Classification), published by WIPO. But the provision of the registration of the design shall be subject to the provision of Section 2(a) and 2(d) of the Design Act.

Reciprocity Application

In the reciprocity treaties with the UK or with any other convention country or a group of countries or inter-governmental organizations, application has to be made within a period of **6 Months** from the date of the first application.

Examination

When the Application for the registration of the Design has been filed, the controller would examine the application just like in case of trademarks and patents we have seen, and further the design application can be registered in not more than one class. If the examination report has been issued, the applicant, if in case there are any objections in the application, has to remove the objections within a period of **3 Months** from the receipt of the date when such examination report has been received by the applicant, or **6 Months** from the date of filing of the application.

The applicant can either himself/herself remove the objections or can take the help of Patent Agent registered in the patent office. If in case no objection has been removed or the reply to the examination has not been filed by the applicant or the agent, then such application shall be treated as **Withdrawn**. Provided that the period to remove the objection shall not exceed more than **6 Months** from the date of filing of the Application for the Registration for Design.

Following would be the process:

Applicant files for the registration of Design.

Examination Report is Issued, if any.

*Applicant files the reply to the examination report circumventing the objections raised in the report within a period of **3 Months** from the date of receipt of the examination report, and that shouldn't extend to more than **6 Months** from the date of filing of the application (R. 18(1) of Design Rules).*

*The applicant may also apply for the Hearing within a period of **3 Months**.*

*If the Controller thinks it's desirable to hear the Applicant, he would appoint a hearing date and the applicant shall be given at least **10 Days** of notice and the applicant or his/her agent has to notify to the controller whether he/she shall attend the hearing.*

After the hearing, the controller may or may not register, or refuse the application for the registration of design application.

*Any application within a period of **6 Months** from the date of the application due to neglect or default of the applicant, shall be deemed to have been abandoned.*

Cancellation Proceedings

The difference between Cancellation & Rectification has already been discussed in the previous book.

A petition to the controller can be made w.r.t. the Cancellation of the registration of design u/s 19.

A copy of it shall be transmitted to the registered proprietor.

*If the registered proprietor intends to oppose it, then he/she shall file the counterstatement within **1 Month** which can be extended upto **3 Months** in aggregate only by a special order of Controller, and shall also send the copy to applicant who has filed the cancellation proceedings.*

*The applicant then has to deliver the affidavit and exhibits in support of the opposition i.e. evidence by way of affidavits to the registered proprietor and to the Controller as well within **1 Month** which can be extended upto **3 Months** in aggregate only by a special order of Controller.*

*The registered proprietor shall then leave the evidence in support of its registration to the applicant and also to the controller after receiving of the evidence filed by the applicant for the cancellation within **1 Month** which can be extended by **3 Months** in aggregate only by a special order of Controller.*

*The applicant would then deliver the copy of the evidence in reply to the registered proprietor and to controller as well, within **1 Month** which can be extended by **3 Months** in aggregate.*

No further evidence shall be left until and unless by the leave of the controller.

If the language is not English, then it has to be translated into the same, a copy of it then to be sent to the either side.

*Note, in all of the above, the time allowed to file the counter-statement or to file the evidence by either side shall be ordinarily **1 Month** but shall not extend beyond **3 Months in aggregate** if in case the petition has been made* *by either party in front of the controller and the controller has decided on the extension in positive, to either sides of the parties. (R. 29(9) of Design Rules)*

*After completion of the above procedures, the controller shall appoint a hearing and shall give to the parties no less than **10 Days** of notice.*

In design also, if either of the party decides to be heard, then it shall send a notice to the controller notifying the same.

*If at the time of the hearing, any of the party needs to refer to any publication that has not been mentioned in any of the above documents, then it shall give to the controller and to the other side notice of not less than **5 Days** that would include publication that the party is seeking to reply to.*

After the hearing, the Controller shall determine its decision and report it to both sides.

Term

The term of the copyright in design would be for the period of **10 Years** which can be further extended upto period of **5 Years** by filing the application for the extension of copyright.

Restoration

The application for the restoration of the registration of design can be made u/s 12 of the Design Act.

To restore the design application, a restoration petition can also be filed by the applicant within a period of **1 Year** from the date on which the design ceased to exist. For the same, the evidence needs to be adduced by the applicant. The controller would consider the application and the evidence adduced, and if he thinks the design application shall not be restored, the same shall be intimated to the proprietor accordingly, and if in case within a period of **1 Month** the applicant doesn't request the controller for the hearing, then the controller shall refuse such application for the restoration of the design. And if in case and after the hearing, the controller is satisfied that the failure to pay the fees was unintentional on the part of the applicant, then the controller shall pass such an order and would restore the application and would notify the same to the applicant.

And if the controller decides for the restoration of the application, then within a period of **1 Month,** the applicant has to pay any additional due fees from the date of the order of the controller, the day restoration petition has been allowed, and the same shall be advertised in the official gazette.

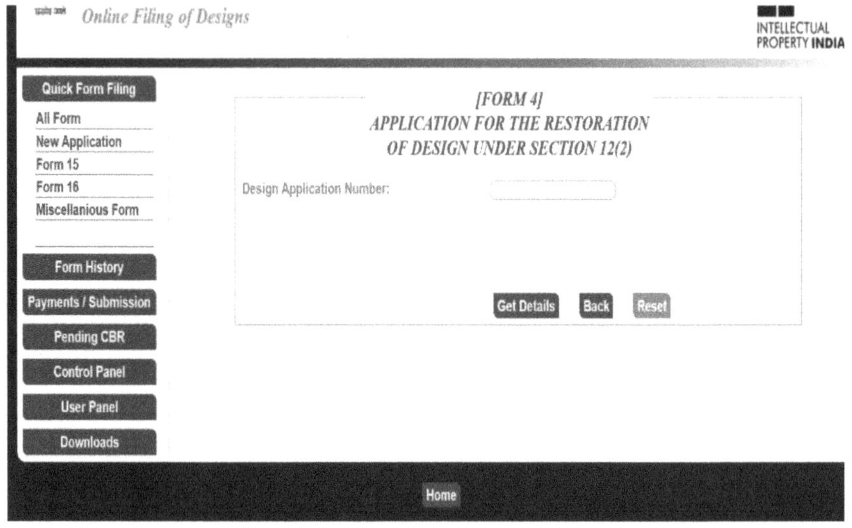

https://online.ipindia.gov.in/eDesign/PATfORMS/desFORM4.aspx

Rectification

In the above case, the application for the cancellation for the design has been filed. Now an applicant can also file an application for the rectification of the register under the Section 31 of the Design Act. Notice the difference, as there are different reasons & grounds for the cancellation petition and the rectification petition. For the ***cancellation***, one needs to prove the following grounds:

> ➤ that the design was previously registered in India;

> ➤ because of its earlier publication or use either within the territory of India or somewhere else;

> ➤ the design applied for isn't original or new;

> ➤ that it isn't registrable under the design act;

> ➤ that it isn't even defined u/s 2(d) to be considered as a design.

WHEREAS,

the rectification petition can be filed on the following grounds:

- ➢ omission or non-insertion of any entry into the register;

- ➢ entry into the register without any sufficient cause;

- ➢ any entry wrongly or erroneously remaining in the register.

Now, when an application for the rectification has been made by the person aggrieved or the ones who have any locus standi, then the controller would serve the same to the people in whose names the registration of the design is registered and would also advertise the same in the official gazette.

*Notice to such application for the rectification can be made within a period of **3 Months** of the advertisement of the application for rectification petition.*

*The opponent within a period of **14 Days** submits relevant statements comprising of all the facts and relief sought.*

The controller then shall furnish the copy of the same to the applicant.

Now, the same process of serving the evidence and exhibits and rely on the earlier publication or notice of the hearing etc. would apply as we have discussed above in the case of cancellation proceedings.

As we have seen, the same process is followed in the case of rectification as has been followed under the proceedings of the cancellation in the design application u/r 29 (4) to 29(13) of the Design Rules.

Thus, in the design act, we have Cancellation & Rectification, for which the reasons are different altogether.

In the trademark section, there is a provision for the opposition and rectification; again, the reasons and grounds for the same are all different. Wherein, in case of trademarks, the application has not yet been registered in the case of the opposition.

Whereas, with respect to patent, there is a provision of the opposition which deals with either the pre-grant or post-grant oppositions and wherein the provision of the rectification petition and the grounds of the pre or post grant oppositions are all different. In case of the pre-grant opposition, the patent application is not recorded in the patent register and the patent certificate is not issued. In case of post-grant opposition, the patent has been recorded in the patent register but the person aggrieved or the ones who have locus standi, can oppose the patent on record within a period of **1 Year** from the date of the grant of the patent.

Now, in case of the trademark, and so as in the case of designs, there is no provision of the compulsory license available, but in the case of the patent and copyrights, there is a provision of compulsory license, given to the person interested.

There are certain discretionary powers that are available to the controller and the controller shall not in the normal course exercise such adversely to the applicant, unless been given an opportunity to the applicant for the same. The same discretionary powers were seen in the case of trademarks also, wherein the registrar can exercise, and also in patents, wherein the controller can also exercise the same.

Thus, if in design, any person wants the controller to exercise any discretionary powers u/s 33 of the design act, then within a period of **1 Month;** the controller shall appoint the hearing to the person exercising such right; which should not be less than or before **10 Days** notice.

Take this example of how to differentiate between a trademark, patent, design and the copyright:

Let us take the example of OMEGA watches:

Trademark-> In OMEGA watches, the trademark consists of the word/ device mark OMEGA. The term would be **10 Years** + recurrence, until renewed.

Patent: In the OMEGA watches, the patent is the unique technology (*functioning feature of the watch*), if any, used inside the OMEGA watches that make their watches to work uniquely. The term would be **20 Years** + annual fees.

Design: The ornamental feature of the OMEGA watch as it appears from the naked eyes and which can be applied in the 2-D or 3-D industrial process. The copyright in design term would be **10 Years + 5 Years extendable**, in terms of the Indian context.

Copyright: Let us say for the booklet or the manual instructions that comes along with the OMEGA watches, or on their website, the images used, or the content included to define the description or the detail about the OMEGA watches or the brand itself and the many other aspects. Copyrights are protected by the reciprocal international treaties. Eg. BERNE Convention, TRIPS, WTO etc. then it would be protected worldwide, whose terms of the protection would change as per the local laws of the country.

And there are classes defined in both the trademarks and the designs, viz. *NICE* classification or the *LOCARNO* classification of goods or services.

Geographical Indications Timeline

As the definition goes in accordance with the act u/s 2(1)(e) of the G.I. act, it means in relation to the goods that determines the geographical origin of those goods, within that particular territory of any country, wherein the reputation and quality of the goods prescribed can be attributed to that particular locality only in that geographical origin, the way those goods are produced, grown, or manufactured, and all that can be associated with that area or locality or particular origin.

For example: Washington Apples, Darjeeling Tea, Mysore Silk, Champane Wines etc.

In the previous book, how the geographical application can be filed, what documentation are required, are already discussed. This book is restricted to the timeline involved in the different procedures under the geographical indication acts and rules.

There're two sections wherein the names are being added in the register: The first is *PART A* wherein the registered proprietor details are being entered, and another is *PART B*, wherein the names and details of the authorized users are added. Herein the register proprietor means any association of persons, or any organization or producers; and not any particular individual or any private entity or otherwise.

The duration of the registration of the geographical indication is **10 Years** which can be renewed subsequently in recurrence; just alike trademark. Similarly in case of the registered user, that can be renewed every **10 Years.**

Restoration

If an application has been made after the period of **6 Months** and within **1 Year** from the period of expiration of the said registration, then the registrar may retore and renew the same, and register it for the period of **10 Years** from the date of the expiration of the said registration. (S. 18(5) of G.I. Act)

If G.I. has been removed for the non payment of the renewal fees, then in spite of that, for any other geographical indication application during the period of **1 Year**, next after the date of the removal, be deemed to be the geographical indication in the register, unless the tribunal is satisfied that:

*1. Non-use of the G.I. that has been removed, within **2 Years** immediately preceding its removal;*

2. No deception would arise with the application removed with another application that is subject to the application for the registration. (S.19)

As already mentioned, that under the trademark registration, there is Section 9(1)(b) which describes the absolute grounds of refusal, wherein if in case the trademark applied under the trademarks act indicate the geographical origin or time of the production of the goods. Now, under the G.I. act such trademarks can be exempted and registered under trademark act if in case and u/s 26.

Furthermore, as seen in the case of trademarks act in case of effect of acquiescence u/s 33 of the trademark act, that if the earlier trademark has acquiesced for a period of **5 Years** in the use of the registered trademark, especially after being aware of it, then, that person or organization shall not be entitled to declare the latter mark against which it has acquiescence, invalid, or to oppose the use of the latter mark, unless the latter trademark was not applied in good faith.

Similarly, no action against the use of any trademark after the expiry period of **5 Years** from the date on which such use or the registration infringes any geographical indication registered under the G.I. act or after the date of the registration of the trademark.

Examination

Every Application of the geographical indication and the statements filed in accordance with rule 32(1), would be examined by the Registrar, within a period of **3 Months** from the date constitution of the consultative group of not more than **7 Representatives** and would issue the examination report to the applicant. If there are any objections raised, then the applicant needs to correct the deficiencies within a period of **2 Months** or apply for hearing, or attend the hearing; else, the application would be treated as dismissed.

The Registrar may withdraw its acceptance before registration if the registrar has any further objections, and if within a period of **30 Days** from receiving such objections, the applicant does not amend its application as the requirement laid down in the further objections, or, does not apply for hearing, the application would be treated as withdrawn. (R.37 of G.I.)

The application of the registration would be ordinarily advertised within a period of **3 Months** from the date of acceptance of the application for advertisement.

Registration of Authorized User

Application of the Authorized User can be filed by any producer u/s 17 accompanied by the statement of the case.

A copy of the application would be forwarded to the Registered Proprietor of the geographical indication (u/r 56 (2) of amendment).

*Where no opposition is filed within **3 Months** extendable to **1 Month** more, in aggregate; or opposition is dismissed; then the Authorized User would be entered in Part B of the register.*

An NOC might also be required from the registered proprietor by the authorized user for its registration.

The opposition timeline is given in the herein followed section.

Falsification of GI

Any person who falsifies or falsely applies to goods any G.I., unless he/she proves was done without intent to defraud, shall be punishable for not less than **6 Months** but which can be extended for a period upto **3 Years.**

Further, there's a penalty for selling goods for which false geographical indication is applied, and the penalty is no less than **6 Months** but may also extend upto **3 Years**, provided further that it may lessened for the adequate and special reasons.

There's also a penalty for falsification of entries in the register, and that shall be punishable with the imprisonment for a term that may extend upto **2 Years** or fine or both.

International Protection

Again, as we've seen that in the case of trademarks, there's Madrid Protocol system or the convention filing of the application in convention nations; in case of patents, there's PCT and Paris convention to protect patents in other nations; in copyright we've seen that they're implicitly protected by the treaties such as BERNE Convention, WTO, TRIPS etc. Similarly, under section 84 of the Geographical Indication Act, there's a special provision for the registration of the application from the citizens of other countries or convention countries.

And according to the Section 85 of the geographical indication act (G.I. Act), wherein no reciprocity is available wherein any country which is a member of the group countries, who does not accord the same privileges to the Indian citizens, as it accord to its own citizens, then nationals of such nations shall not be entitled to apply for the registration of geographical indication in India, nor be entitled to apply for the registration of authorized users.

Opposition

Now, there's also a provision of opposition to the registration of the geographical indication just like we have seen in case of trademarks.

Process would be as followed:

Within a period of 3 Months which shall not be extendable to more than 1 Month in aggregate, if the registrar deems fit i.e., total is 4 Months, any person can give the notice to the registrar from the date of the advertisement or readvertisement of an application for the registration.

The registrar shall serve the copy of notice of opposition within a period of 2 Months onto the applicant of the registration, and within a period of 2 Months from the receipt by the applicant of the copy of notice of opposition, the counterstatement needs to be filed, failing which the application shall be termed as abandoned.

The registrar shall then serve the counterstatement, if filed, to the opponent within a period of 2 Months.

Then the evidence stage would commence, and the opponent would file the evidence within a period of 2 Months from the date of receipt of the counterstatement and which shall not further exceed to 1 Month in aggregate as and if the registrar may allow. The evidence can be either *filed along with exhibits sworn on the affidavit, or, the opponent can rely on statements made in the notice of opposition; and the same what was sent to registrar, the opponent shall send to the applicant as well within a specified period of time. And the extension that has been sought for further period of **1 Month** has to be made in advance before the expiration of the **2 Months** period as mentioned above. If the evidence is not filed, then the opposition shall be termed as abandoned.*

This rely on the pleadings made in the notice of opposition we have also seen in the trademarks, wherein u/r 45(1), the opponent can also rely on the statements made in the notice of opposition if the opponent doesn't want to adduce any evidence via cogent exhibits.

*Then within a period of **2 Months** and not exceeding **1 Month** in aggregate if filed for the extension before the expiration period of **2 Months**, the applicant can file its evidence in support of application or can rely on the facts made in the counterstatement, from the date of receipt of the evidence, or, rely letter filed by the opponent; and the same shall be served to the opponent and to registrar as well.*

*After receipt of the evidence filed by the applicant, the opponent can then file the evidence in Reply within a period of **1 Month** which shall not be exceeding to **1 Month** more in aggregate, and leave the evidence with the registrar and concurrently send the same to the applicant.*

After the above stages are completed, then no further evidence would be allowed to be filed except with the leave of registrar.

*Upon completion of the evidence stage, within a period of **3 Months** the registrar shall send the notice to the parties for the hearing, wherein the date of hearing shall be not less than **1 Month** from the date on when such notice was first issued. And within a period of **14 Days** the parties who intend to attend the hearing shall notify the registrar about his/her intention for attending. And if either of the party fails to notify the registrar, then the matter would be decided ex-parte.*

*The matter can also be adjourned on the request, subject to that no more than **2 Adjournments** would be granted within the gap of no more than **1 Month** each.*

If the Applicant fails to appear for the hearing, then the application would be considered as abandoned, and if the opponent fails to appear for the hearing even after the adjournment, and also fails to notify the registrar about intention to attend the hearing, then the opposition would be treated as dismissed on the want of prosecution.

The Rules herein are followed from Rules 41 to Rule 50 of the geographical indication rules; wherein in the case of trademarks, the Rules for the opposition hearing was included under Rule 42-51 of the trademark rules. The procedure is almost similar, except in case of the timelines.

Renewal

The renewal of the registration of G.I. has to be made not more than **6 Months** before the expiration of the last registration of the geographical indication mark or of the authorized user.

Now, as stated that the renewal has to be filed by the registered proprietor of the geographical indication mark. As per the **rule 60(5)**, where the registered proprietor has ceased to exist, then, *the renewal of the registered geographical indication shall be effected by any of the authorized users of the registered geographical indication acting collectively whose name has been entered in **Part B** of the register on the due date of renewal.*

Now, a notice of the same has to be issued by the registrar, to the proprietor or to authorized user of the geographical indication before their removal; which shall be made not less than **1 Month** and not more than **3 Months** before the expiry of the expiration of last registration.

If the renewal fee has not been paid to the Registrar by the proprietor of the geographical indication or by the authorized user, then the mark or user shall be removed from the register, and the same would be advertised in the journal.

But, if in case before within a period of **6 Months** of cease, the said fees has been paid along with surcharge, then the geographical indication or the authorized user shall not be removed.

Rectification

Similar to that of trademarks, there's also a provision of rectification in the geographical indication register. The process that needs to be followed is:

A copy of the rectification of the geographical indication or of an authorized user, a petition made u/r 65 & Section 27 of geographical indications act and rules, shall be made to the registrar and the registrar would serve the same *onto the registered proprietor and to any person interested or whoever are in the register within a period of **2 Months.***

*Within a period of **2 Months** and that should not be extended for further **2 Months** in aggregate, from the receipt of the copy of such application of rectification, he/she shall send the copy of counterstatement to the registrar.*

*The registrar shall within a period of **1 Month** serve the copy of counterstatement to the person making the application of the rectification.*

And as mentioned in the opposition section of filing of the evidence stages and hearing, i.e. provision of rules 44 to 51 shall apply. But the mark or the user shall not be rectified merely for the reason that the registered proprietor or the registered user has not filed the counterstatement provided that the non-filing on the part of either or both, was justified or reasonable reason was given.

The registrar can also rectify the register on his/her own motion, and within a period not less than **1 Month** from the receipt of the notice sent by the registrar in writing, the registered proprietor needs to send the facts he/she relies upon, and within that period an application for the hearing can be made.

For any discretionary powers u/s 61, the person entitled be **1 Month** from such a notice that registrar has given before determining the matter, and the registrar would give no less than **10 Days** of notice if within that period that person is required to be heard. (R. 84)

Now, the person aggrieved can also file for the Review petition against the Registrar's decision within a period of **1 Month** from the date of such decision, which can be extended for a period of **1 Month** more in aggregate, if the registrar may allow.

And the Appeal from the decision of the Registrar shall be filed within a period of **3 Months.** (R. 98)

Domain Name Disputes

The details about the domain names disputes have already been discussed in the previous book. Where gtld and cctld petitions can be filed, in case of an act of Cybersquatting.

Either the person aggrieved can reach to the local jurisdiction in the court of law for remedy, or, can choose UDRP (Uniform Domain Name Dispute Resolution Policy) route to get appropriate order after filing of the complaint against respondent (*against whom complaint has been filed*), or in case of cctld domains, can approach via INDRP route.

Mostly while applying for the registration of domain name with the Registrar (eg. GoDaddy etc.), you apply on *first come first serve* basis only. There's no procedure of examination or of examination report being issued or objections raised or filing of reply to the examination report or rectification or opposition within a prescribed timeline, in the case of registering of domain names.

Thus, domain names, when it comes to an act of cybersquatting, is a grey area, wherein anyone can get registered anything, if it's being available online or if in case the holder of domain name has not renewed his/her domain; as one has to pay annual fees for its renewal and to keep it protected.

Everyone is abided by the agreement executed between the parties. For instance, Registrant-Registrar; Registrar-ICANN, Registry-Registrar etc.

Mostly, gtld related domain name complaints' in case of cybersquatting are filed at UDRP, but in certain cases, cctld related domain name disputes in case of cybersquatting can also be filed directly with UDRP.

Certain terms & definitions needs to be remembered:

Respondent: *Against whom the complaint has been filed*

Complainant: *The person aggrieved who is filing the complaint*

Reverse Domain Name Hijacking*: An attempt to deprive the domain name holder rights using the said policy*

Registrar*: The entity that registers domain name and with whom the Respondent has registered its domain name (eg. GoDaddy)*

Panel*: the administrative panel appointed by Provider who would decide the complaint, by Panelist*

Provider*: Dispute resolution service provider who would appoint the panel and panelist(s) who decide on a complaint*

Registrant*: A person in whose name the domain name is registered, that can be complainant or respondent*

Now, when the complainant identifies the respondent against whom the complaint would be filed for the act of cybersquatting, it has to be sent electronically

Your Complaint and any annexes should be submitted by email to: domain.disputes@wipo.int. File size and format specifications are set out in WIPO Supplemental Rules.

https://www.wipo.int/amc/en/domains/complainant/index.html

https://www.wipo.int/domains/en/filing/response

The complaint shall include the registrar where the respondent's domain name is registered, details about the complainant, details of respondent wherever it's possible, specify the domain name against which the complaint has been filed, specify the trademarks which is basis of the complaint in the act of cybersquatting, remedies sought, action required at the earliest, annexures, and all the cogent exhibits on which complainant relies upon, etc.

Once the complaint has been sent electronically, the provider shall submit a verification request to the Registrar with whom domain name is registered and it would also include to Lock the domain name.

*Within **2 Days** from Provider's request, Registrar shall provide Provider the request details in the verification request and shall put a Lock of the domain name and would confirm the same to Provider.*

The Lock applied on the domain name remains as long as the pendency of the UDRP proceedings.

*The Provider now go through the Petition filed and if it's in compliance with the policy and rules, then it will forward the same complaint to the registrar and to the respondent as well, within a period of **3 Calendar Days** from the receipt of fees paid by the Complainant.*

*If in case there's any deficiency in the complaint; provider shall notify the complainant and to the respondent about the same, and the complainant shall have **5 Calendar Days** to correct the deficiencies; else if not done in the said period of time, the complaint shall be treated as withdrawn, and following the same, the provider shall notify the registrar, and then the Lock on the domain name shall be removed/released by Registrar within a period of **1 Day.***

If the above things go without any deficiencies, then the administrative proceedings shall commence.

*Within **20 Days** from the date of the commencement of the proceedings, Respondent has to submit its response, which can be further extended upto **4 Days.***

The Respondent would send all the cogent exhibits along with the facts and statements and documents in the Response.

*If neither of the complainant nor the respondent has provided the number of Panelists, i.e. **3 Member Panel,** then within the period of **5 Days** the provider shall appoint **1 Panelist** in the Panel.*

If the Provider has elected 3 Panel Members on the request by the Complainant, then the Complainant has to pay fees in the entirety.

And if the Respondent elects 3 Panel Members, then the fees would be split equally between the parties. i.e. between the complainant and respondent.

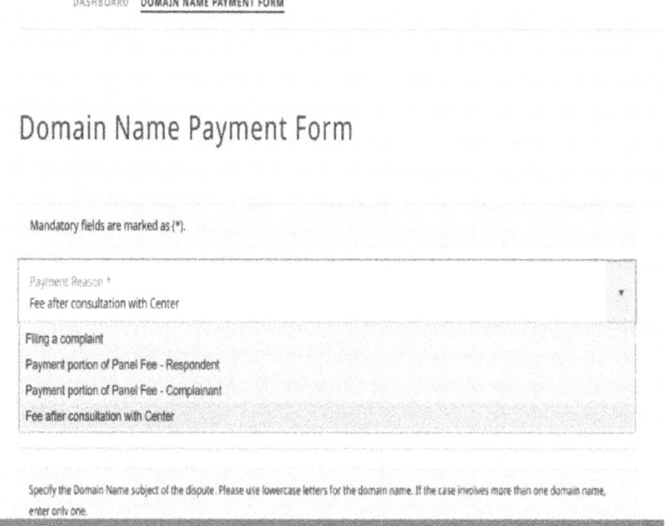

https://www3.wipo.int/amc-payment/dn-form

All the communications would be made via the case administrator appointed by the Provider.

The Provider shall forward the file to the Panel as soon as the panelists are being appointed.

There shall be no in person hearing, unless the Panel considers it appropriate.

*The Panel then forwards its decision within a period of **14 Days** to the Provider. In the decision, it may also consider the reverse domain name hijacking arguments if made by the Respondent.*

*The Provider shall within **3 Days** forward the decision of the Panel to Parties involved i.e. to the Complainant, Respondent, Registrar, and to the ICANN as well.*

*The Registrar shall implement the decision within a period of **3 Days** received from the Provider.*

*The decision would be available on the website. And if before the Panel's decision, a settlement is reached or made by the parties, then the Panel would terminate administrative proceedings. And if there's any outcome of the settlement, then the Registrar shall remove the Lock within a period of **2 Days** from the date of receiving the notice from the Provider about the settlement reached. And after the settlement, the complainant would confirm the Provider about the implementation of the settlement, and the Provider would dismiss the proceedings.*

*If the Provider does not receive the fee from the Complainant within a period of **10 Days,** then the complaint shall be deemed as withdrawn.*

The Provider and the Panelist won't be liable for any of the act or omission in connection with the administrative proceedings.

Wherein:

The INDRP (.IN Domain Name Dispute Resolution Policy) rules, where proceedings in case of cybersquatting involves cctld domain names *viz.* **.in / .bharat**. As in case of UDRP, there're several cctld domain names that are also being included in the UDRP now, the list of which is available on WIPO web portal.

Thus, as discussed in the previous book, in case of gtld domain names, if prosecution being filed from India, then one has to select UDRP proceedings; and in case of cctld domains in which **.in** or **.bharat** domains are included, then one has to apply via INDRP prosecution. This is also beneficial, in terms of the cost proceedings, as in case of UDRP we've seen that electing of even a single panelist would cost around **1, 500/- USD**, which is expensive if being compared to the national arbitrator, which would be approx. **35,000/- INR**. In case of UDRP, one has to file at the WIPO, wherein in case of INDRP, one has to file the complaint at NIXI which is the National Internet Exchange of India. One of the main features of INDRP is that the Complainant has to pay the entire fees, and not the Respondent, unlike in case of the UDRP policies that if the Respondent elects 3 Member Panelists, then the fees would be divided into half, paid both by the Complainant and Respondent.

In case of no email is available on the registry.in of the Respondent, then the complaint is sent on *postmaster @ the contested domain name.* The same thing is as discussed in the previous book, if in case due to privacy feature is enabled, the details of the respondent are not available, then there too the complaint would be sent to the postmaster @ contested domain name. Else, other remedies are also being discussed in the previous book.

Further, the INDRP policy has been adopted by NIXI.

The complaint has to be submitted in the electronic form to NIXI.

The complaint shall be evaluated and if in case of any objections, within a period of 5 Days would be notified to the complainant and then within a period of 7 Days the complainant needs to submit the rectified complaint.

An Arbitrator would be appointed within a period of 5 Days and would notify to the parties involved.

Then, within 2 Days, complainant sends the accepted copy of complaint electronically as a soft copy to Arbitrator appointed, and to the respondent as well. The complaint shall be of not more than 5000 Words excluding annexures, and not more than 100 Pages in total.

The complainant has to abide by the final award binding arbitration conducted in accordance of Arbitration & Conciliation Act.

The Arbitrator issues notice to the Respondent within 3 Days from the receipt of the complaint from the complainant.

The Arbitrator shall conclude proceedings within a period of 60 Days which can be further extended to 30 Days from the date of commencement of the proceedings.

Within 30 Days the party can raise an objection in case of any clerical or typographical error in the Award.

The registrants/complainants/respondents would've to indemnify the NIXI, .IN Registry, Registrar, and the Arbitrators.

Personal hearings, as in case of UDRP also, are being conducted only in the rarest of the rare circumstances.

The award would be communicated by the .IN Registry within 5 Days to all parties.

The Registry cannot transfer the domain name in the following situations:

> ➤ *Unless the arbitration hearing has been completed and an award has been granted for the same;*

> ➤ *If the arbitration proceedings are pending;*

> ➤ *Unless a settlement has been reached between the parties concerned i.e. the Complainant & Respondent and the same has been notified to all parties concerned including NIXI, Arbitrator, .IN Registry;*

> ➤ *In case arbitration proceedings are completed, then a period of **90 Days** from the passing of such an award;*

> ➤ *In the event of wherein the award has been challenged by either party, till the pendency of such proceedings.*

But if in case there's any breach or violation occur w.r.t. rules, then the Registry would reserve the right to transfer the domain.

Thus, the difference between the UDRP and the INDRP is, as in the latter case, an Award is being granted under the Arbitration & Conciliation Act, wherein the former, under the UDRP Rules & Policy. Furthermore, an Arbitrator is appointed in the case of latter; whereas in case of the UDRP, the number of Panel members are being chosen by the Complainant or Respondent (1 or 3), and if in case of 3 Panel members chosen by the Respondent, then the fees is shared equally between the Complainant & Respondent; wherein in the case of the INDRP, the fees is paid by the Complainant only. Furthermore, the timeline in case of the UDRP is slightly lesser than in case of INDRP. In case of the UDRP, it's *generally* restricted to the gtld domain names, but in the case of INDRP, the domain names are restricted to ***.in or .bharat.***

References

82

1. Professional Publisher Bare Acts of Patents, Trademarks, Copyrights, 2023
2. www.ipindia.gov.in (Designs / G.I.)
3. www.wipo.int (UDRP, MADRID PROTOCOL / REGULATIONS, PCT)
4. www.copyright.gov.in
5. www.registry.in
6. www.nixi.in

About The Author

Pranav Chaturvedi has a decade of exposure in IPR domain. He's also registered with Bar Council of Maharashtra & Goa, and has furthermore published SIX books (five of which are collection of his poetries and Epic poetries (*No Tenets, Species Another, We All Become Philosophers Sooner Or Late, Epic Six Poetries, In The Quest of Essence of Soul & Sand*), and one on the IPR subject domain viz. *IP For Everyone: Ethics, Filing, Reflections* which are available on different online platforms as well as in stores. He's also a blogger, poet, who has published several hundreds of blogs, e-books & poetries on his blog portals:

www.jpranavc.com ,

www.jpranavc.in

www.jpranavc.blog

www.jpranavc.medium.com

www.jpranavcip.com